To krupa
The best cake
Maker ever a
you really are a
brilliant cake maker
always make them
uhh you do
Butterfly

PENGUIN BOOKS

THE BIG BOOK OF TREATS

Pooja Dhingra is the founder of Le15 Pâtisserie and Studio Fifteen Culinary Centre in Mumbai. A graduate of Le Cordon Bleu, Paris, she brought a piece of that world to India through her delectable desserts and a beautiful cafe. She has been featured in national dailies and is a regular in fashion and lifestyle glossies not just for her abilities in the kitchen, but also as a dynamic businesswoman and inspiration to women—she was selected by *Forbes* India for their 30 under-30 entrepreneurs list. She has been voted a Rising Star by GC Watches and is featured in its global campaign.

The menu at Le15 Pâtisserie has been praised in several prestigious publications—Indian and international—while Bollywood stars, sportspeople, corporate czars and politicians are regular clients. She loves coffee, chocolate and sepia-toned Instagrams, as much as coming up with new collaborations and business ideas to make Le 15 Pâtisserie a brand to reckon with.

POOJA DHINGRA

THE BIG BOOK
OF TREATS

PHOTOGRAPHY BY CYRUS DALAL

PENGUIN BOOKS

PENGUIN BOOKS
Published by the Penguin Group
Penguin Books India Pvt. Ltd, 7th Floor, Infinity Tower C, DLF Cyber City, Gurgaon 122 002, Haryana, India
Penguin Group (USA) Inc., 375 Hudson Street, New York, New York 10014, USA
Penguin Group (Canada), 90 Eglinton Avenue East, Suite 700, Toronto, Ontario, M4P 2Y3, Canada
Penguin Books Ltd, 80 Strand, London WC2R 0RL, England
Penguin Ireland, 25 St Stephen's Green, Dublin 2, Ireland (a division of Penguin Books Ltd)
Penguin Group (Australia), 707 Collins Street, Melbourne, Victoria 3008, Australia Penguin Group (NZ), 67 Apollo Drive, Rosedale, Auckland 0632, New Zealand
Penguin Group (South Africa) (Pty) Ltd, Block D, Rosebank Office Park, 181 Jan Smuts Avenue, Parktown North, Johannesburg 2193, South Africa

Penguin Books Ltd, Registered Offices: 80 Strand, London WC2R 0RL, England

First published by Penguin Books India 2014

10 9 8 7 6 5 4

ISBN 9780143422686

Designed by Haitenlo Semy
Printed at Replika Press Pvt. Ltd, India

To Mom, Dad, Vaarun and Viddhi

CONTENTS

ACKNOWLEDGEMENTS

On 28 November 2012 I updated my Facebook status saying, 'I would love to write a recipe book. My mother says if you truly want something put it out in the universe. So, there, Universe, please do your thing!'

Within minutes, my friend Chinmayee sent me a message saying, 'Pooja, I join Penguin in February, and I'm going to call you then.'

What started out as a joke to annoy my mother ended up making one of my biggest dreams come true.

This book would not have been possible without the following people. I thank all of them from the bottom of my heart for being my support system, my guinea pigs and my encouragement, and for helping me see the light when I couldn't.

Mom, Dad and Vaarun: For being my pillars, for letting me have crazy dreams and always encouraging me to follow my heart.

Chinmayee: For making this happen and for all the coffee to keep me going.

Lata Bua: Thank you for introducing me to the magical world of baking!

Rachana: For being my sounding board, helping me find my voice and being the greatest friend a girl could ask for.

Maitri: This book is as much yours as it is mine. Thank you for your time, effort, patience and efficiency. Thank you for pushing me and making sure I stuck to all my deadlines. I truly couldn't have done this without you.

Cyrus: For being supportive throughout the process. Thank you for putting up with my fickle mind and for shooting (and re-shooting) everything.

Pratish: For everything, always.

Kamini: Dolly, thank you for having my back. I am lucky and blessed to know someone like you.

Ann, Pinank and my Le15 family: For being the best team. For helping me test and re-test each recipe. For letting me take time off from the kitchen and focus on writing this book.

Marie: I would never have gone to Paris if it wasn't for you. Thank you for being you, for all the long walks and talks. All your help in the early stages of setting up Le15 allowed it to become what it did. And for that, I am ever grateful.

Daniel: For moving to Mumbai, for testing recipes, taking photos, being a great friend and confidant and most importantly—for believing that we could create something wonderful.

Aditi: For all the joy and sunshine in my life. For being my partner in crime for 20 years and always pushing me to be my best.

Martin: I'm doing what I love and you helped me get here. Thank you for always believing in me.

Pankil and the team at The Pantry, Mumbai: For allowing us to shoot at your beautiful café and making sure we always had enough caffeine.

Thank you, **Sonia Faleiro**. You were the first person I ever told I wanted to write and you showed me the way.

A big shout-out to **Jenai**, **Melanie**, **Mitalee**, **Purva**, **Kamal**, **Philipp**, **Henry**, **Jill**, **Carol**, **Ankit**, **Carolina**, **Pablo**, **Radhika**, **Jash**, **Yashna**, **Kadam**, **Priti**— you have all inspired recipes in this book, and I am ever so grateful for having you in my life.

Thank you **Mr London**, **Tarsila**, **Catherine Baschet**, **Mr Rochoux** and all my chefs from **Le Cordon Bleu Paris** for helping me shape my career.

And thank you **Ameya, Gavin, Paloma and the Penguin team** for your help and contribution to making this book.

HELLO!

By the time this book goes to press, I would have run a professional pâtisserie for four years. When I look back to the day I graduated from Le Cordon Bleu, Paris, it seems like I've been on the clichéd long journey, but also like I've been caught up in a whirlwind. From discovering baking at home as a little girl to turning out macarons and cupcakes for thousands, the ability to whisk flour, butter and sugar together has brought me much, much joy and learning.

I am a big believer in working hard towards making your dreams come true and when I see them unfolding in front of my eyes, I always say a silent prayer in gratitude. Over the years, I have been fortunate enough to earn friends, supporters, fans and fame through baking. My work has brought me so much happiness but, more than that, what my staff and I turn out every day at the kitchen brings immense joy to the customers that support Le15—whether they buy a choux pastry on their way home from work, order cakes for special occasions or ask me to set up counters at their weddings.

I've been fascinated with baking for as long as I can remember. My first proper kitchen memory is from when I was seven years old. It was the day my aunt taught me how to make brownies. I was amazed that simple ingredients like eggs, butter, sugar and flour could create something so delicious and magical. As I grew older, I continued experimenting with desserts. I remember obsessively crushing biscuits and adding condensed milk and cocoa powder to them. I called it cocoa delight.

To me, baking is the only thing that makes perfect sense in a world that never is—or can, or should be—perfect. The kitchen at Le15 Pâtisserie is my favourite place. I am at peace with the buzz of whisking and the aroma of baking. I have to confess that it still surprises me how much I feel at home in a kitchen, when it was never any part of my professional plans growing up.

I quit law school to study hospitality management in Switzerland, where I started to discover who I really was. As an intern in a pastry kitchen, I loved the smell of chocolate cookies as they came out of the oven and, most of all, I enjoyed using my hands to create something beautiful and delicious. That was when I knew what I wanted to do.

So I moved to Paris to study at one of the best culinary schools in the world— Le Cordon Bleu. It's funny to think now that I didn't know what a macaron was until I ate my first passion fruit macaron in Paris at 21. My fondness for food also comes from the realization that flavours play on your palate and become memories. Now every time I have a passion fruit macaron, I am transported to that windy day in Paris, when I stood outside the pastry shop and bit into my prized purchase.

At school in Paris, we learnt the importance of techniques, and witnessed different ways in which the same 'magic ingredients' can be used to achieve such a huge variety of treats. During my internship at a chocolate shop I absorbed the work ethic, the amount of time and effort that goes into running a business. My chef was the first person in the shop at 6 a.m. and the last person out at 8 p.m. every single day. I knew that this was the level of dedication I would need when I started baking professionally.

When I moved back to India, I was so excited to try making everything that I had learnt in France. But I had been away for five years and realized just how different things are in Indian kitchens. It wasn't only the difference between a professional kitchen and a home kitchen; it was the availability of ingredients, the weather, the equipment . . . well, everything! I started tweaking recipes for my home kitchen and, using mostly local ingredients, I managed to create some pretty amazing desserts. I started baking for friends and family and they loved everything that came out of the little oven at home. At the same time,

I knew that if I wanted to contribute to the pastry scene in the country, I needed to take bigger steps and started looking for a kitchen space while working on creating a brand.

My vision was clear: I wanted to recreate a piece of my life in Paris. I wanted to make wonderful desserts, using the best ingredients I could find and serve happiness in a box. And that is how Le15 (named for the 15th arrondissement in Paris, the neighbourhood where I lived) was born.

Writing *The Big Book of Treats* has brought one journey full circle for me. When I was 16, I wanted to bake cookies at home one day. My mother said that I couldn't use eggs on that day, and I had to look online for a recipe for eggless cookies. It was then that I wished I had a book with me that suited Indian kitchens and their traditions, which would tell me how to make some-thing special for a birthday but also something ordinary to have with masala chai in the afternoons.

Here's the thing. As a baker I have two personalities. The first is when I am in the Le15 kitchen supported by fancy ovens, hi-tech equipment and a team to work with. The second is when I am baking at home with ingredients purchased from a shop around the corner, with no shiny equipment—only my modest little oven staring back at me. But then, at home, not many—including me!—have the time and the means to bake like a professional. And that's where this book comes in. I have written this book as a home baker, but with a professional baker's exacting eye.

The Big Book of Treats is steeped in my culinary philosophy: simple techniques, subtle flavours and comforting, delicious desserts that anyone can make. Baking is not a skill that's traditionally taught in an Indian kitchen and the idea behind this book is to help anyone at any age bake with accessible ingredients and easy techniques. You can choose to start with very approachable recipes, such as vanilla cupcakes (page 125), or take the challenge on head first with macarons (page 205). However, whether you are beginning or continuing your own baking journey with this book, I really wish for each reader to experience that sense of achievement when you are done frosting a cake or baking the perfect tart. And, of course, that sense of comfort and happiness when you share it with friends and family and create memories that will come back to you every time you bake.

Good luck!

Le15, Bandra

BAKING 101

INGREDIENTS

The biggest problem I had while growing up was finding unsalted butter, double cream, heavy cream, sour cream, vanilla extract . . . you get my drift. It really wasn't easy to find ingredients. Luckily things have changed and most ingredients are available in large cities, though I still have a problem paying an arm and a leg for a slab of unsalted butter. While working on this book, I did my best to use ingredients that are easily available in local stores. So should you.

Butter: I use regular Amul butter in all the recipes, which have been created taking into account the salt and moisture content of the butter.

Flour: Local maida. Make sure to always sift flour before using it.

Milk: All the recipes use whole milk. You can use either the tetra pack or the packet milk that is more commonly available—both are good choices.

Eggs: I use regular farm eggs in the recipes. Some people prefer to use organic eggs which are now available in large supermarkets. Again, choose whatever you are good with.

Cream: Most recipes that use cream require fresh cream—I use the Amul tetra pack.

Whipped cream: When a recipe calls for whipped cream, I use either Tropolite or Rich non-dairy whipping cream. To be able to whip cream it must have a fat content of more than 30 per cent, which is very difficult to find here. You could get cream from the local dairy and whip that as well. When you do this make sure that the bowl is clean and that it has been in the freezer for 15 minutes, because cold utensils will get you better results.

Castor sugar: Finely granulated sugar that is easily available in most shops. When a recipe asks for castor sugar, try not to use regular sugar. Thicker granules will not melt in the batter thoroughly and will change the texture of the recipe. Powdered sugar will not be able to hold the cake up and you might find your cake sinking once out of the oven. There are different brands of castor sugar available in most cities. In Mumbai we use Bluebird or Marwana and in Delhi, Solar is a popular brand.

Brown sugar: Demerara sugar, easily available in most stores. Again, go with a popular brand like Bluebird, Marwana or Solar.

Chocolate: My favourite brands of cooking chocolate are Valrhona and Callebaut. If they are not easily available, I am fond of Morde, Indian cooking chocolate. The kind of chocolate you use really depends on the role it is playing in a recipe. For instance if you are making a molten chocolate cake (page 76), where chocolate is your star ingredient, then use the best that's available to you. For a recipe like chocolate chip cookies (page 19) or a flavoured truffle, Indian cooking chocolate works just fine.

Baking powder vs baking soda: Okay, this is very simple. All you need to know is that they are both leavening agents. They help release carbon dioxide when added to baked goods which helps our pretty cupcakes and cakes to rise.

So when do you use which?

Baking soda is pure sodium bicarbonate. When the recipe has acidic ingredients (yogurt, buttermilk, chocolate), baking soda reacts with them under oven temperatures and helps the cake rise. This is a very quick reaction, so batters with baking soda should be baked immediately and not stored, or they will fall flat.

Baking powder contains sodium bicarbonate, cream of tartar (acid factor) and a drying agent and is used mostly in neutral batters (when you're using milk for moisture for example). You can substitute baking powder for soda, but not the other way around.

Vanilla beans/extract/essence: I worked under a chef who loved adding vanilla to everything and that habit stuck with me. Vanilla extract is hard to find but you can make your own by steeping split vanilla beans in vodka and storing the container in a cool dry place for a minimum of 6 weeks.

Vanilla beans are now easily available in India—I source mine from Kerala. These are very potent and one bean can be used to flavour around 2–3 litres of cream/liquid. To use the bean, split it in half vertically and use a small knife to scrape out the innards and use them in your dessert. Instead of throwing away the beans, add them to your sugar jar and enjoy vanilla flavoured sugar.

Vanilla essence is made from artificial ingredients to recreate the vanilla flavour.

Cocoa powder: In my kitchen I use Dutch processed cocoa powder. This kind of cocoa powder is specially treated to lower acidity, change colour and be more soluble in liquids. It works well with recipes that use baking powder, as most recipes in this book do.

At home, you can use either a natural or Dutch processed cocoa powder. Different brands of cocoa powder are available in the market, such as Bluebird, Hershey's, Cadbury or Callebaut.

EQUIPMENT

The single most important thing you need—I can't tell you how important it is—is an accurate weighing scale. Please get one; it is impossible to bake without it. Baking is a science and every gram counts. You will also need:

Mixing bowls: Medium-sized round bowls will work for most recipes. I always use stainless steel ones because they are lightweight and easy to clean and to store.

Whisks: These recipes are written for someone using a hand balloon whisk. You can use an electric whisk or a stand mixer with a whisk attachment.

Spatulas: I stock my pantry with silicon spatulas. They are flexible and help get that last drop of chocolate out of any bowl.

Baking paper/parchment paper/Silpat: Baking paper or parchment paper is also known as butter paper. It has a greaseproof surface and is usually disposable. I highly recommend buying a Silpat (silicon baking sheet). It may be slightly expensive but it's long-lasting and very easy to maintain.

Moulds: Depending on which recipe you follow you will need cake tins, tart rings, mini tart moulds, a spring form tin (for cheesecake), a bread tin (for loaf cakes) and square moulds (brownies).

Foil and cling wrap: Most cookie dough needs to be cling-wrapped and refrigerated before baking. Foil can be used as a substitute for baking paper while baking cookies. For cakes that take long to bake—as loaf cakes do—covering your tin with foil helps prevent the top from burning.

Piping bags and nozzles: I like using piping bags to pour batter into moulds—it is cleaner and hassle free. You could use a spoon or spatula to do the same. Using piping bags requires some practice but, once mastered, it makes baking much easier. It is important to use a piping bag and nozzle when decorating cupcakes. My preferred nozzles are star nozzles (sizes 8–10) for cupcakes and round nozzles (sizes 10–12) for macarons.

TECHNIQUES

Beating/Whisking till light and fluffy: Most recipes will call for this. This is a very important step in baking because it is at this stage that we incorporate air bubbles into our batter. Baking powder or soda can only enlarge existing air bubbles and doesn't introduce new ones. Ideally, one should spend 2–3 minutes whisking the butter and sugar with an electric beater or 4–5 minutes if using a hand whisk to get the desired result.

Sifting: Passing the flour through a sieve is a vital step. It helps aerate the flour and you are certain it doesn't have any impurities. Baking powder and flour should always be sifted or whisked together because you want the baking powder to be evenly distributed in your cake for an even rise and don't want a soapy clumpy chunk of baking powder in your mouth when you bite into a treat.

Folding: This is a process we use to incorporate a lighter mixture into a denser one. Folding is gentler than mixing. Most recipes call for the flour to be folded into the batter. The things to remember while folding flour are:
• Mix in one direction.
• Use a spatula with a gentle hand. If you use a whisk and beat vigorously you will activate the gluten in the flour which will make the cake a lot denser.

Melting chocolate: There are two ways you can do this. The chef at the chocolate shop I worked at used to tell us that 'chocolate is allergic to water and gas'. He didn't let us melt chocolate directly on the flame, because chocolate burns easily. So I use a DOUBLE BOILER OR HOT WATER BATH, in which a bowl is placed on top of a pan of simmering water. The steam from the water helps melt the chocolate and there is no direct heat. This is a controlled method where you are certain the chocolate won't burn. You could also melt chocolate in the microwave, by putting it in a microwave-safe bowl and taking it out and stirring it every 15–20 seconds until it is completely melted. Here the risks of burning are higher.

Lining/Greasing a baking tin: My mother always greased her baking tins—it's a good trick for home chefs. Greasing a tin involves running some soft butter all around the sides and the bottom and then dusting it with flour. At school we learnt how to line the tins using baking or parchment paper. With paper, you are certain your batter will not stick to the tin. It is easier to remove the baked goods from the tin and place them on a flat surface to cut. Butter paper or parchment paper does not need greasing.

To line a tin, measure out baking paper 2 inches bigger than the width of your tin. Cut a 2-inch slit at all the edges so you can easily fit it inside the tin.

GENERAL TIPS AND TRICKS TO HELP YOU BECOME A SUPER BAKER

Don't keep opening the oven door! Opening it for 30 seconds can drop the temperature drastically. Be patient.

Adding flavour to the fat helps distribute it better. If a recipe calls for vanilla, add it to the butter to get a more intense flavour.

Roasting enhances the flavour of nuts.

Use a clean bowl to beat egg whites. Any traces of yolk in the whites and you won't be able to whisk them stiff.

Wrapping tart/cookie dough in plastic wrap and refrigerating it for a minimum of 2 hours helps moisture to distribute evenly.

Store baking powder or soda in an airtight container in a dry place to keep it potent.

Chocolate needs a lot of love and has to be stored correctly. If it is kept in very hot temperatures for a long time, it blooms—fat and cocoa butter float to the top.

Stir chocolate constantly while melting to keep the temperature even.

Always read the recipe thoroughly before starting.

Measure all your ingredients and lay them out before you.

Once you're a bit comfortable with a base recipe, try and experiment with flavours.

And last, always, always, ALWAYS remember to have fun!

CONVERSION TABLE

PRODUCT	1 CUP	½ CUP	¼ CUP
Flour	120g	60g	30g
Butter	220g	110g	55g
Castor Sugar	220g	110g	55g
Brown Sugar	200g	100g	50g
Icing Sugar	120g	60g	30g
Liquid	200g	100g	50g

1 Tablespoon: 15g	1 Teaspoon: 5g

COOKIES

BARS

BROWNIES

This is probably the most special and nostalgic section of the book for me because I've been baking cookies and brownies since I was a little girl. Cookies, brownies and bars are really the simplest and most rewarding things to bake. For a first-time baker, these recipes are the least intimidating while being a great way to learn the art.

The good thing with most cookie dough is that you can make and freeze it for as long as you need to. So when that craving kicks in, all you do is cut, shape and bake! The bonus is that cookie dough always tastes better when it's had time to rest in the fridge/freezer. The flavours are more intense and you get a controlled spread.

I prefer my cookies a bit gooey in the centre and crisp on the edges. To achieve this, pull the cookie tray out 2 minutes before the baking time is up and transfer them to a cooling rack.

The majority of the recipes are my favourites, and I have updated different techniques and methods for the classic ones. This means that each recipe has variations. I recommend that you try them all out and find the one that works best for you.

COOKIES

Nutella squares, page 42

Peanut butter brownie cups, page 49

Jam thumbprint cookies, page 23

Double chocolate chip cookies, page 30

CHOCOLATE CHIP COOKIES

Makes 20 medium-sized cookies

This classic recipe is one of my favourite things to bake!
At university in Switzerland, I would make a batch of these
every other weekend and realized that they made for perfect
presents too.

I've used 2 kinds of sugar in this recipe because I like each
one's texture and what they bring to the table. If you prefer
to use either one, that should work fine too.

Ingredients	Method
75g butter	Whisk together the butter, brown sugar, castor sugar and vanilla essence till soft and fluffy
65g brown sugar	
50g castor sugar	
1tsp vanilla essence	
1 egg	Break the egg in, whisking properly after each addition
1tsp baking powder	Sift the baking powder and flour and fold it into the mixture with a spatula
175g flour	
175g dark chocolate, chopped	Mix in the dark chocolate chips. Now cling wrap and refrigerate the dough for at least 2 hours

Preheat the oven to 165C and either grease your baking tray
with butter or line it with parchment paper

With a tablespoon, scoop out the dough on to the baking tray in
medium-sized rounds, leaving a 2-inch gap between each cookie

Bake for 15 minutes or till the edges start browning

BUTTER COOKIES (EGGLESS)

Makes 30 cookies

Simple, buttery and melt-in-your-mouth, these cookies are brilliant comfort food. Once you are comfortable making these, you can play around with flavours. Add some cinnamon instead of vanilla, or lemon zest or even crushed pepper if you're feeling adventurous.

200g butter
125g castor sugar
1tsp vanilla essence
250g flour

In a bowl, whisk together the butter, castor sugar and vanilla essence till soft and fluffy

Fold in the flour with a spatula

Take a piece of cling film and place the dough across the middle

Make a log shape by rolling the dough gently inside the cling film and then refrigerate it for 2 hours

Preheat the oven to 165C and either grease your baking tray with butter or line it with parchment paper

Cut the dough into medium-sized pieces and lay them on the tray

Bake for 15 minutes or till the edges start browning

PEANUT BUTTER COOKIES

Makes 25 medium-sized cookies

Peanut butter is one of my great loves. So, of course, I had to put it in these deliciously crumbly cookies. The brown sugar adds a caramelized flavour, and the peanut butter lends crunch. These are best eaten fresh out of the oven.

....

75g butter
115g brown sugar
75g chunky peanut butter
1 egg
½tsp baking powder
125g flour

Preheat the oven to 165C

Whisk the butter, brown sugar and peanut butter together in a bowl till soft

Add the egg and whisk properly till combined

Sift the flour and baking powder together

Add to egg mixture, using a spatula to fold it in

Line your baking tray with parchment paper

With a tablespoon, scoop out the dough on to the baking tray in medium-sized rounds, leaving a 2-inch gap between each cookie

Bake for 15 minutes or till the edges start browning

WHITE CHOCOLATE CORNFLAKE COOKIES
Makes 25 cookies

Roasting the cornflakes in this recipe keeps them crisp even after baking. You could add some walnuts, butterscotch or even chopped apricots to the dough to lend additional texture and taste. Though I confess I love them with just cornflakes and white chocolate.

150g butter
200g castor sugar
1tsp vanilla essence
2 eggs
1tsp baking powder
250g flour
100g cornflakes
50g white chocolate, chopped

Put the cornflakes on a baking tray and bake at 165C for 5–7 minutes, till crisp

Whisk together the butter, castor sugar and vanilla essence till light and fluffy

Add the eggs one at a time, whisking well after each addition

Sift together the baking powder and flour and fold into the mixture with a spatula

Add the cornflakes and white chocolate and mix well

Preheat the oven to 165C and either grease your baking tray with butter or line it with parchment paper

With a tablespoon, scoop out the dough on to the baking tray in medium-sized rounds, leaving a 2-inch gap between each cookie

Bake for 15 minutes or till the edges start browning

JAM THUMBPRINT COOKIES

Makes 20 medium-sized cookies

These cookies are best had with your evening cup of tea. You can use the jam of your choice. This is a great recipe to bake with a group of friends or, even, with kids. I remember baking these with my mom when growing up and we always had fun.

Ingredients	Method
100g butter	Whisk together the butter, castor sugar and vanilla essence till light and fluffy
120g castor sugar	
1tsp vanilla essence	
1 egg	Add the egg and whisk well
½tsp baking powder	Sift together the baking powder and flour and fold into the above mixture with a spatula
175g flour	
50g jam	Mix till you get a dough and refrigerate for 2 hours
(any flavour of your choice)	

Preheat the oven to 165C and line your baking tray with parchment paper

Take small quantities of the dough, make small balls and flatten with your fingertips into medium-sized cookies

Put them on the baking tray, leaving a 2-inch gap between each cookie. Using your thumb, make small wells in the middle of each cookie

Put a teaspoon of jam in each well

Bake for 15 minutes or till the edges start browning

Once cool, top the wells with some more jam and serve

HAZELNUT MERINGUE COOKIES (GLUTEN FREE)

Makes 12 cookies

Give me anything with hazelnut and I'm happy. Clearly, this is a popular opinion because at Le15 Pâtisserie, too, our hazelnut-flavoured goodies fly off the shelf. Plus, these cookies are light and don't have any flour, which makes them perfect for those with gluten allergies. I prefer using a star nozzle for this recipe, but you could use any that you choose.

Tip: You could substitute the hazelnuts with almonds to make almond cookies.

100g hazelnuts, powdered
80g icing sugar
1 egg white
½tsp cinnamon
A pinch of salt

Preheat the oven to 180C

Put the powdered hazelnuts, icing sugar, egg white, cinnamon and salt in a bowl and whisk together to combine

Once it has formed a stiff batter, pipe it on to a baking tray lined with parchment paper, leaving a 2-inch gap between each cookie

Bake for 10 minutes or until the edges start browning

OAT COOKIES (EGGLESS)

Makes 20 medium-sized cookies

I use fresh grated coconut in this recipe because it's easy to find and adds a great texture to the cookies. This recipe is eggless and doesn't require any baking. Easy peasy!

....

60g dark chocolate, chopped	Melt the dark chocolate, butter and honey and leave to cool
20g butter	
1 ½tbsp honey	
75g oats	When cool, add the oats and fresh grated coconut and mix till incorporated
50g freshly grated coconut	
1 ½tbsp cocoa powder	Add the cocoa powder and mix to form a batter
	Make medium-sized rounds and refrigerate till set

PEANUT BUTTER AND
MILK CHOCOLATE COOKIES
Makes 20 cookies

These cookies are perfect to satiate any peanut butter cravings. I like them best made with chunky peanut butter. The milk chocolate adds to the texture, but if you're impatient like me, I suggest eating them hot out of the oven.

125g castor sugar
50g brown sugar
200g peanut butter
½tsp vanilla essence
1 egg
50g flour
70g milk chocolate

Whisk together the castor sugar, brown sugar, peanut butter and vanilla essence till fluffy

Add the egg and whisk till incorporated

Fold in the flour into the mixture with a spatula and mix till you get a dough

Refrigerate for 2 hours

Preheat oven to 165C and line your baking tray with parchment paper

With small quantities of the dough, make medium-sized balls and flatten them with your fingertips and place on the baking tray

Leave a 2-inch gap between each cookie

Bake for 12–15 minutes or till the edges start browning

Melt the milk chocolate over a hot water bath

Once cool, dip the cookie in the melted chocolate and leave it to set before serving

TAHINI COOKIES

Makes 45 cookies

This is my friend Daniel's recipe. Daniel and I were in culinary school together in Paris. When he was visiting me in Mumbai we would often end up spending the entire day in the kitchen, experimenting and exchanging ideas. Of all the things he baked, this cookie was my absolute favourite! It is quite unusual and I love that it is not too sweet.

I find tahini easily at local stores in Mumbai, but if you have a hard time finding it all you need to do is lightly toast a cup of sesame seeds in the oven or in a pan. Once cool, mix with 2 tablespoons of vegetable oil and a pinch of salt. Add some warm water and blend till you get a smooth paste.

100g butter, softened
240g castor sugar
320g flour
180g tahini
2tsp lemon juice
50ml milk
200g sliced almonds
50g whole almonds

Mix the butter, castor sugar and flour with your hands till the mixture looks like breadcrumbs

Add the tahini and lemon and mix properly

Add the milk to get a doughy consistency

Finally, add the almonds and mix well

Make small balls and flatten them with your fingertips and place them on the baking tray leaving a 2-inch gap between each cookie

Make a small depression on top of each cookie and press one whole almond onto each depression

Bake at 165C for 15 minutes or till the edges start browning

GINGER SPICE COOKIES (EGGLESS)

Makes 30 cookies

This recipe is for those who like some spice even in their desserts. I love the ginger in this recipe but if you feel like it's too pungent, just use cinnamon. Otherwise, they are perfect with your morning cup of adrak chai.

....

200g butter
125g castor sugar
250g flour
2tsp fresh ground ginger
1tsp cinnamon powder
1tsp nutmeg powder

In a bowl, whisk together the butter and castor sugar till soft and fluffy. Fold in the flour with a spatula

Add in the ground ginger, cinnamon powder and nutmeg powder and mix till you get a dough

Take a piece of cling film and place the dough across the middle. Make a log shape by rolling the dough gently inside the cling film and then refrigerate the dough for 2 hours

Preheat the oven to 165C and line your baking tray with parchment paper

Cut the dough into medium-sized pieces and lay them on the tray

Bake for 15 minutes or till the edges start browning

16-YEAR-OLD CHOCOLATE CHIP COOKIES (EGGLESS)

Makes 35 cookies

When I was 16 years old, I was obsessed with this recipe. It all started on a particular Tuesday when Mum wouldn't allow me to cook with eggs at home. I started researching a recipe that I could bake without eggs and I have been using this one ever since. The trick with these cookies is to remove them from the oven when they are slightly undercooked and allow them to cool on the baking tray. You can make this recipe into an oatmeal and raisin cookie by simply replacing the chocolate with raisins.

180g butter
135g brown sugar
60g castor sugar
1tsp vanilla essence
250g flour
1tsp baking soda
30ml boiling water
75g quick cooking oats
200g dark chocolate, chopped

In a bowl, whisk together the butter, castor sugar and brown sugar

Add the vanilla essence and whisk well. Fold in the flour

Add boiling water to the baking soda and pour into the dough. Mix well

Finally, add the oats and chocolate

Wrap the dough in cling film and refrigerate for a minimum of 30 minutes

Make small balls and flatten with your fingertips

Preheat your oven to 165C for 10 minutes and then bake for 10–12 minutes

DOUBLE CHOCOLATE CHIP COOKIES

Makes 40 cookies

Wafer-thin and very crisp, these cookies really differ from the other recipes in this book. I love the combination of dark and milk chocolate but if you don't, just use one kind. Or, substitute the milk chocolate with white. I sometimes add butterscotch chips in the batter to make it much more decadent.

175g dark chocolate, chopped
50g butter
50g flour
¼tsp baking powder
2 eggs
250g castor sugar
1tsp vanilla essence
100g milk chocolate, finely chopped

Preheat oven to 180C. Line a baking sheet with parchment or butter paper

Melt the dark chocolate and butter together either in the microwave or in a double boiler and cool

In a bowl, beat the eggs, castor sugar and vanilla essence till thick and pale

Stir in the melted chocolate

Sift the baking powder and flour and add to the mixture along with the milk chocolate

Drop tablespoons of the mixture on to the baking sheet leaving a 2-inch gap between each cookie and bake for 8–10 minutes

Let them cool before you transfer them into a container

TRIPLE CHOCOLATE CHIP COOKIES

Makes 30 cookies

If you are as addicted to chocolate as the rest of us, this one is for you. I often make a batch of these when I am invited to people's homes and I can tell you that it's made me a very popular guest. If you're hosting, crumble these up and use as a topping for ice cream for a quick and easy dessert that's sure to please.

....

250g butter
200g brown sugar
1tsp vanilla essence
1 egg
350g flour
150g dark chocolate, chopped
100g milk chocolate, chopped
100g white chocolate, chopped

Whisk together the butter and brown sugar till the mixture is pale and thick

Add the vanilla essence and egg and whisk till combined fully

Fold in the flour and chocolate chips with a spatula and make the dough

Make small balls and flatten with your fingertips into medium-sized rounds and place on the baking tray leaving a gap for 2 inches between each cookie

Bake at 160C for 10 minutes

CINNAMON CHOCOLATE CHIP COOKIES
Makes 25 cookies

Marie, my French friend, has a very different approach to baking cookies. She beats the egg directly into the butter instead of beating the butter with sugar. This way the brown sugar crystals are visible and add a crunch to the cookie. Try her trick while baking these.

250g flour

85g castor sugar

165g brown sugar

1tsp baking powder

1 egg

1tsp cinnamon

180g butter

200g chopped dark chocolate

Sift together the flour, castor sugar, brown sugar and baking powder

Whisk the egg and cinnamon together

Melt the butter and, when it has come to room temperature, add the egg and whisk

Fold the flour mix into the butter mix with a spatula

Add the chocolate chips, mix and make a dough

Cling wrap the dough and refrigerate for 30 minutes

Make small balls and flatten with your fingertips into medium-sized rounds

Bake at 180C for 8–10 minutes

BARS

FRUIT AND NUT BARS (EGGLESS)

Makes 10 bars

Extremely easy to bake—when we made these in our kitchen we couldn't stop eating them. The best part: they are eggless and don't even need an oven!

450g dark chocolate

225g butter

200g chopped roasted almonds

150g chopped raisins

300g digestive biscuits

Melt together the dark chocolate and butter

Add the chopped roasted almonds and chopped raisins and mix properly

Break the digestive biscuits into pieces and mix into the batter

Pour into an 8-inch lined baking tin and refrigerate for 2 hours or till set

Let it cool in the tin and then cut into bars and store in an airtight container for up to 2 weeks

Dark chocolate fudge bars, page 39

Hazelnut cheesecake brownie, page 48

Granola bars, page 41

Chocolate chip cookies, page 19

DARK CHOCOLATE FUDGE BARS
Makes 10 bars

Who didn't grow up eating homemade fudge? It's such a comforting snack, and I've updated it by using dark chocolate. Its brownie-like texture just adds to the mix. Make a batch for when you're spending an evening at home, or take it with you on weekends away.

100g butter
75g dark chocolate
2 eggs
250g castor sugar
2tsp vanilla
½tsp baking soda
200g flour
75g roasted almonds, chopped
75g white chocolate chips

Melt together the dark chocolate and butter. Set aside to cool

Whisk the eggs, castor sugar and vanilla till light and fluffy and add into the mixture and whisk

Sift together the flour and baking soda and fold into the mixture with a spatula

Add the almonds and white chocolate chips and mix till combined

Pour into an 8-inch lined baking tin and bake at 180C for 20 minutes

Let it cool in the tin and then cut into bars and store in an airtight container for up to 7 days

WHITE CHOCOLATE AND
DRIED APRICOT CRUNCH (EGGLESS)
Makes 10 bars

I like the combination of white chocolate and apricot but you could use dates, raisins, butterscotch chips or even dried cranberries. This recipe doesn't require any baking and is a good one to make with kids.

250g white chocolate
25g butter
40g rice puffs
150g dried apricots, chopped

Put the rice puffs in a saucepan and toast till crisp

Melt together the white chocolate and butter in a double boiler

Add the rice puffs and the chopped apricots and mix

Put into an 8-inch lined baking tin and refrigerate for 2 hours or till set

Let it cool in the tin and then cut into bars and store in an airtight container for up to 2 weeks

GRANOLA BARS (EGGLESS)

Makes 10 bars

A great snack to make and store for a few days. It also makes for a pretty gift and I can vouch that most people love these for the healthy ingredients.

150g butter
60g brown sugar
60g honey
175g muesli
75g oats
100g deseeded, chopped dates

In a saucepan/microwave, melt the butter, brown sugar and honey together until well combined

Remove from heat and stir in the muesli, oats and deseeded chopped dates

Transfer to an 8-inch lined tin and bake at 190C for 18–20 minutes till slightly golden

Let it cool in the tin and then cut into bars and store in an airtight container for up to 5–7 days

NUTELLA SQUARES (EGGLESS)

Makes 10 squares

There's a self-imposed ban on these squares for me. Because the first time I made them I ate so many that I had to police myself. Be warned!

75g dark chocolate	In a microwave, melt the dark chocolate and butter and leave aside to cool
125g butter	
50g brown sugar	
100g flour	Add the brown sugar and whisk till combined properly
75g oats	
400g Nutella	Fold in the flour with a spatula and then add the oats and mix
100g chopped roasted hazelnuts	

In a microwave, melt the dark chocolate and butter and leave aside to cool

Add the brown sugar and whisk till combined properly

Fold in the flour with a spatula and then add the oats and mix

Preheat the oven to 180C and either grease an 8-inch baking tin with butter or line it with parchment paper

Bake for 15–20 minutes

Once cool, spread the Nutella evenly on top and garnish with the chopped roasted hazelnuts

PEANUT BUTTER FUDGE BARS (EGGLESS)

Makes 6 bars

Another simple no-bake recipe. I like to add some cinnamon powder and chocolate chips when I'm making these for myself.

....

100g chunky peanut butter
100g butter
1 tsp vanilla essence
200g icing sugar

In a saucepan, heat the peanut butter, butter, vanilla essence and icing sugar. Whisk till thick. If it is not thick enough, add some more icing sugar

Once thick and slightly cool, pour into a 6-inch baking tin lined with butter paper and refrigerate for 2 hours or until set

Let it cool in the tin and then cut into bars and store in an airtight container for up to 1 week

NUTTY GOOEY STICKY
FUDGE BARS (EGGLESS)
Makes 20 bars

This fudge is my pick-me-up on rough days. I love that it is so easy to make. Try using the best kind of chocolate you can find for this recipe since chocolate is the star ingredient here. There are several changes you can make to this: add a different kind of nut, or chocolate chips, desiccated coconut, crushed Oreo biscuits, butterscotch chips and more. Let your imagination take over.

500g dark chocolate
200g cream
15g butter
100g almonds and cashew nuts, chopped and roasted

Melt the dark chocolate over a double boiler or in the microwave

Heat the cream and butter in a saucepan over medium flame, till it boils

Pour this over the melted chocolate and slowly whisk till combined

Stir in the chopped, roasted almonds and cashew nuts and mix well

Pour into an 8-inch baking tin lined with butter paper and refrigerate for 2–4 hours or until set

Use a knife dipped in hot water to cut the fudge

BROWNIES

ALMOND WALNUT BROWNIE

Makes approximately 24 pieces

....

400g dark chocolate, chopped
200g butter
3 eggs
200g brown sugar
1 tsp vanilla essence
½tsp baking powder
80g flour
75g roasted almonds, chopped
75g roasted walnuts, chopped

Melt the dark chocolate and butter together

Whisk the brown sugar and eggs till light and fluffy and add the vanilla essence

Add the chocolate mixture to the egg mixture

Sift flour and baking powder and fold in with a spatula

Add the chopped almonds and walnuts and mix lightly

Bake in a 9-inch tin lined with butter paper for 25–30 minutes

Once cooled, cut into squares and serve

Preheat oven to 165C

CHOCOLATE WALNUT BROWNIE

Makes approximately 20 pieces

....

One of the first things I ever baked was a batch of these. Brownies are comforting, simple and the easiest way to win someone over. If you make a larger batch, freeze them for a rainy day. Most people love to eat a warm brownie with a scoop of ice-cream but they're also delicious cold on a summer evening.

115g butter
150g milk chocolate, chopped
80g dark chocolate, chopped
2 eggs
120g brown sugar
80g flour
1 tsp baking powder
75g roasted walnuts, chopped

Preheat oven to 180C

Melt the dark chocolate, milk chocolate and butter together in a double boiler and leave to cool

Whisk eggs and brown sugar together. Add to the chocolate mixture and whisk well

Sift the flour and baking powder and fold into the chocolate mixture with a spatula

Add the walnuts and mix lightly

Bake in an 8-inch tin lined with butter paper for 20–25 minutes

Once cool, cut into squares and serve

HAZELNUT CHEESECAKE BROWNIE

Makes approximately 36 pieces

This has two of my favourite desserts: brownies and cheesecake. It couldn't get better, right? But it does, with hazelnut of course. These are gorgeous, highly addictive and the perfect dessert to bake for that special someone. You will have them eating out of your hands, literally.

FOR THE BROWNIE
250g butter
250g dark chocolate, chopped
5 eggs
350g castor sugar
1 tsp vanilla essence
100g flour
50g hazelnut powder
(roast some hazelnuts and once they are cool, blend them in a mixer for a minute)

FOR THE CHEESECAKE
175g Philadelphia Cream Cheese
2tbsp castor sugar
1 egg
25g cream
15g flour

Line a 10-inch tin with butter paper and preheat the oven to 180C

To prepare the cheesecake batter, in a bowl, whisk the cream cheese and castor sugar till smooth. Then add the egg and cream and whisk till combined. Lastly, add the flour and give a final whisk. Set aside

Melt the dark chocolate and butter together and leave to cool

Whisk eggs, castor sugar and vanilla till frothy. Do not over-whisk

Pour the cooled chocolate mix into the egg mix and whisk till combined

Add flour and hazelnut powder to the chocolate mix and fold it in with a spatula

Pour into a baking tin and then swirl in the cheesecake mixture (use a skewer to get the pattern you desire)

Bake for 22–25 minutes. The centre should be slightly wobbly Once cool, cut into squares and serve

PEANUT BUTTER BROWNIE CUPS

Makes approximately 24 cups

I recommend warming these in the microwave for a brief 30 seconds and then topping them with vanilla ice cream. You can replace the peanut butter with Nutella, caramel or chocolate, according to your preferences. Again, note that it is better to use chunky peanut butter.

125g castor sugar
75g butter
15ml water
250g dark chocolate, chopped
1 egg
1tsp vanilla essence
150g flour
½tsp baking soda
125g peanut butter
125g chocolate chips (optional)
35ml milk

Preheat oven to 180C and line a mini cupcake baking tray with liners

Melt the dark chocolate, butter and castor sugar with water in a microwave and set aside

Once cooled, add the egg and vanilla essence and whisk well

Sift the flour and baking soda and fold into the mixture with a spatula

Add the milk and the chocolate chips and mix lightly

Spoon the batter into the liners and bake for 10–12 minutes

Once done, they would have sunk a little in the middle. If not, make a slight depression in the middle with the back of a spoon and fill it with peanut butter and top with chocolate chips

RED VELVET BROWNIE

Makes approximately 20 pieces

It took a while to adapt my most popular cupcake recipe into a brownie. But what is life without challenges? These brownies are excellent for gifting at festivals.

70g butter

160g castor sugar

45g dark chocolate

2 eggs

1tsp vanilla essence

1½tsp red food colour

105g flour

½tsp baking powder

(Cream cheese frosting on page 148)

In a bowl, beat the eggs, castor sugar and vanilla essence till light and fluffy

Melt the butter and dark chocolate together in a microwave and add to the above mixture

Add the red food colour and mix

In a bowl, sift together the flour and baking powder

Add it to the chocolate mixture and mix with a spatula till incorporated

Bake at 180C for around 18–20 minutes in a lined 8-inch tin

Once cool, cut into squares and serve

CAKEY BROWNIE

Makes approximately 20 pieces

If you prefer your brownies a bit cakey and less gooey or fudgy, this recipe is for you. Up the ante by using this as a sponge cake base for ganache or buttercream.

85g butter
120g castor sugar
85g brown sugar
125g dark chocolate
2 eggs
85g flour
15g cocoa powder
½tsp baking powder

Melt together the butter, castor sugar, brown sugar and dark chocolate in a microwave and set aside to cool

Once cooled, whisk the eggs and add into the chocolate mixture

Sift together the flour, cocoa powder and baking powder and fold into the mixture with a spatula till incorporated

Bake at 180C for 20 minutes in a lined 8-inch baking tin

Once cool, cut into squares and serve

NUTELLA BROWNIE

Makes 24 pieces

Is there anything more sinful than Nutella on brownies? Take my word for it, there isn't! I am partial to hazelnuts but you could use walnuts or any other nuts that you like in this recipe.

170g butter
150g dark chocolate
85g white chocolate
15g cocoa powder
350g castor sugar
3 eggs
70g flour
100g chopped hazelnuts
¼ tsp baking powder
150g soft Nutella

Preheat the oven to 180C

Sift together the flour and baking powder

Over a hot water bath, melt the butter, dark chocolate and white chocolate. Mix with the cocoa powder and set aside to cool

Whisk the castor sugar and eggs till light and fluffy

Slowly pour the melted chocolate mixture over the eggs and whisk well. Be careful not to over-mix

Fold in the flour, followed by the chopped hazelnuts

Spread the batter in a greased 9-inch baking tray

Bake for 30 minutes or till a skewer comes out clean

Once the brownies have cooled down a little, generously spread the Nutella over them and cut to the desired size

BLONDIES
Makes 20 pieces

Blondies are bars made with the basic ingredients—butter, sugar, flour and eggs. They have a different consistency from brownies and may contain chocolate chips. I use this recipe quite often and like the crunch of the butterscotch, brown sugar and chocolate chips.

....

100g butter, melted
200g brown sugar
1 egg, lightly beaten
1tsp vanilla essence
½tsp baking powder
¼tsp baking soda
120g flour
⅓ cup (60g) butterscotch chips, chopped walnuts, chocolate chips

Preheat the oven to 175C and line an 8-inch tin with butter or parchment paper

Whisk together the melted butter and brown sugar in a bowl till light and fluffy

Add the egg and vanilla essence and whisk

Sift together the flour, baking powder and baking soda and fold into the above mixture

Mix the butterscotch chips, chopped walnuts and chocolate chips into the batter

Pour into the baking tin, spread evenly and bake for 25 minutes

Molten chocolate cake, page 73

White chocolate and rose sponge cake, page 70

Chocolate ginger cake with rose ganache frosting, page 66

Classic chocolate cake, page 72

CAKES

When you say baking, you think cake. This section pays homage to the different techniques and kinds of cake—from a classic sponge to a cheesecake to cakes for special occasions. A cake is such a classic dessert and, if you start with the most basic recipe, you can invent a signature as you go along.

BAKED CHEESECAKE

I first made cheesecake in university, when my Malaysian friend Kamal taught me how. It opened up a whole new world when he showed me how easy it is. As I made more types of cheesecakes, I realized that I prefer baked cheesecakes to set ones. This cake tastes better the next day once it has had time to cool.

There are only two important things to look out for when making a cheesecake: Overmixing the batter, and opening the oven door from time to time once the cake is inside. Don't do that because your cake will crack. You want the cake to still be slightly wobbly in the centre once you pull it out of the oven as it will keep cooking for a few hours thereafter. If you do see some cracks, we have a wonderful cream cheese frosting to hide them!

CRUST

150g digestive or Marie biscuits
50g butter, melted

FILLING

400g Philadelphia Cream Cheese
1tbsp lemon juice
175g castor sugar
55g cream
A pinch of salt
½tsp vanilla essence
3 eggs

(Cream cheese frosting on page 148)

Crumble the biscuits in a food processor or crush with a rolling pin

Put in a bowl and then add the melted butter and mix

Line the base and sides of a 9-inch spring form cake tin with the biscuit mix and press it with the back of a spoon to spread evenly
Bake for 10 minutes at 165C and let it cool

In a bowl, beat the cream cheese till fluffy

Add the lemon juice, castor sugar, cream, salt and vanilla essence

Add the eggs one at a time, mixing well after each addition.
Pour the mixture into the cooled crust

Bake at 165C for 40–45 minutes or till you see the sides brown lightly

MANGO CHEESECAKE (EGGLESS)

This is my mother's cheesecake recipe that she often makes at home. I get nostalgic about this one because it reminds me of lazy May vacations at home and days filled with delicious food. I use Alphonso mangoes because they feel like summer to me. You could use other varieties of mango that you prefer, or even strawberries or kiwis instead. Make this your own recipe filled with your own stories.

CRUST
200g digestive biscuits
50g butter
50g castor sugar

FILLING
200g Philadelphia Cream Cheese
200g condensed milk
100g whipping cream
1 tbsp lemon juice
25g gelatin
¼ cup water

GARNISH
Sliced mangoes

(Variations: Garnish with sliced strawberries, cherries or use blueberry topping.)

Crumble the digestive biscuits with a rolling pin or food processor

Melt the butter in a saucepan and add the digestive biscuit crumbs and castor sugar to it. Mix well and remove from the stove

Line the base and sides of a 9-inch spring form cake tin with a removable base and press it with the back of a spoon to spread evenly

Bake at 165C for 5–7 minutes. Set aside to cool

Whisk cream cheese and condensed milk with a blender

Beat the cream till thick and add to the cream cheese mixture. Fold in the lemon juice

Mix the gelatin with water and heat, stirring all the time till the gelatin dissolves completely. Remove from the stove and set aside to cool. Strain it through a sieve

Add the cooled gelatin in a thin stream to the mix, making sure to whisk well so there are no lumps

Pour this into the prepared tin. Cover and chill in the fridge for 4–6 hours. Place on a serving plate and garnish with sliced mangoes

CONDENSED MILK AND CARDAMOM CAKE (EGGLESS)

The flavour of cardamom reminds me of a particular kind of biscuit I used to eat as a child. I find this cake extremely comforting and love eating it warm from the oven with my cuppa. I prefer to bake it like a pound cake and then slice it before serving, but you could bake the batter as cupcakes, a loaf or even sandwich layers of this cake with a cream cheese frosting.

200g condensed milk
125ml milk
100g butter
15g castor sugar
125g flour
½tsp baking soda
1tsp baking powder
2tsp cardamom powder

Whisk together butter and castor sugar till light and fluffy

Add the cardamom powder and mix

Add the milk and condensed milk and whisk till mixed well

Sift together the flour, baking soda and baking powder and fold into the above mix with a spatula

Bake at 180C for 20–22 minutes in a lined 6-inch cake tin

CHOCOLATE GINGER CAKE WITH ROSE GANACHE FROSTING (EGGLESS)

In Paris, I worked in a chocolate shop that made a lemon ginger chocolate, which I found very interesting. I always felt it needed some tweaking, though. Ginger has a glorious flavour but when I started experimenting with it in my cakes I felt I needed something to balance the 'pepperiness' of the root. Finally, I decided to use a rose ganache as frosting to add the necessary sweetness.

200g condensed milk
125ml milk
100g butter
15g castor sugar
125g flour
½tsp baking soda
1tsp baking powder
150g melted dark chocolate
1tsp fresh grated ginger
2tsp ginger juice

(Rose ganache frosting on page 150)

Whisk together butter and castor sugar till light and fluffy

Add the milk and condensed milk and whisk till mixed well

Add the melted dark chocolate and whisk

Add the grated ginger and ginger juice and mix

Sift together the flour, baking soda and baking powder and fold into the batter with a spatula

Bake at 180C for 20–22 minutes in a lined 6-inch cake tin

CHAI CAKE (EGGLESS)

Masala chai keeps me going through my hectic days. It is no easy feat perfecting that cup, but my team at Le15 gets it right every time. Once while working on a new menu I asked one of them to make me a cup without sugar and I used that in a cake. The result was fantastic: the subtle flavours of chai in a rich sponge cake. It's soothing and hits the spot every single time.

200g condensed milk

125ml chai (made with milk and without sugar)

100g butter

15g castor sugar

125g flour

½tsp baking soda

1tsp baking powder

Whisk together butter and castor sugar till light and fluffy

Add the condensed milk and chai and whisk till mixed well

Sift together the flour, baking soda and baking powder and fold into the batter with a spatula

Bake at 180C for 20–22 minutes in a lined 6-inch cake tin

CARROT CAKE

I'm a big fan of carrot cake. I usually go hunting for the best carrot cake in whichever city I visit. That said, it is very easy to make, and I feel like I am eating something healthy! I like using a cream cheese frosting with a little bit of lemon zest to break the sweetness. Toasted walnuts add an excellent crunch to this cake.

3 eggs
150g brown sugar
200g flour
1 tsp vanilla essence
1 tbsp baking powder
1 tsp cinnamon powder
½tsp ground ginger
150ml vegetable oil
60g curd (hung, drained of excess water)
350g carrots, grated
150g walnuts, chopped and toasted

(Cream cheese frosting on page 148)

Preheat the oven to 165C

Beat the vegetable oil and brown sugar together

Add the curd and continue to whisk

Add the eggs one at a time, whisking well after each addition

Sift the flour and baking powder and fold into the above mixture along with the cinnamon powder and ground ginger

Add the carrots and walnuts and mix well with a spatula

Pour the batter into a 7-inch cake tin and bake for 40–45 minutes

HAZELNUT CAKE (GLUTEN FREE)

A friend of mine at university suddenly found out that she had become intolerant to gluten. As a baker this was a nightmare come horribly true and it completely changed her life. I adapted a recipe for her without flour, using her favourite hazelnuts instead. Nut flours are a bit dense and do leave a bit of oil. But they make for absolutely delicious desserts! You could substitute the hazelnut powder with almond powder and perhaps even add some chocolate chips to make it more sinful.

....

125g butter	Whisk the butter and castor sugar together till thick
200g castor sugar	
1tsp vanilla essence	Add the vanilla essence and whisk
3 eggs	Add the eggs one at a time till each one is combined
250g ground hazelnuts	
	Add the ground hazelnuts and mix with a spatula
	Bake in an 8-inch tin at 165C for 20 minutes

WHITE CHOCOLATE
AND ROSE SPONGE CAKE

This is an extremely pretty cake and would make the perfect centrepiece for any little girl's birthday party.

60g ground almonds
120g butter
150g castor sugar
100g white chocolate
1tsp rose essence
3 eggs
125g flour

(Rose buttercream frosting on page 149)

Melt the butter and white chocolate together in a microwave and set aside

Beat the eggs and castor sugar till thick and add the rose essence and whisk

Add this mixture to the chocolate mixture and whisk

Add the flour and the ground almonds and mix with a spatula

Bake in an 8-inch tin at 165C for 20 minutes

Once the cake has cooled, slice it in half and spread some of the buttercream on it. Sandwich the layers and then let the cake cool in the fridge for an hour. Then, use the rest of the buttercream with a piping bag and a star nozzle to decorate it.

BEETROOT CAKE (EGGLESS)

Beetroot is such a common—but unpopular—Indian vegetable and this recipe gives it a glamorous makeover. The sweetness and nutritional value of beetroots make this cake quite special. Plus, it's eggless so win-win all the way.

150g condensed milk
25ml milk
100g butter
15g castor sugar
125g flour
½tsp baking soda
1tsp baking powder
150g dark chocolate
2 small beetroots, boiled and puréed

Preheat the oven to 180C

Melt the dark chocolate in a microwave and leave aside to cool

Whisk together butter and castor sugar till light and fluffy

Add the milk and condensed milk and whisk till mixed well

Add the melted dark chocolate and whisk

Slowly add in the beetroot purée and mix well till combined properly

Sift together the flour, baking soda and baking powder and fold into the batter with a spatula

Bake for 20–22 minutes in a lined 6-inch cake tin

CLASSIC CHOCOLATE CAKE

If you ever feel like baking your own birthday cake (I know I always do!) this recipe should help you out. It's a basic chocolate sponge with 2 different frosting ideas. You could use buttercream or a ganache to layer this cake. The method remains the same for both. Decorate with sprinkles or chocolate shavings.

SPONGE

4 eggs

160g castor sugar

140g dark chocolate

70g flour

30g cocoa powder

(Chocolate buttercream frosting on page 151)

(Chocolate ganache frosting on page 159)

Preheat the oven to 180C

Melt the dark chocolate in a microwave and set aside to cool

Whisk the eggs till light and fluffy. Add the castor sugar and keep whisking till the sugar dissolves

Add the cooled dark melted chocolate to the mixture and fold in lightly. Be careful not to over-mix

Sift together the flour and cocoa powder and add to the mixture

Pour into a lined 8-inch baking tin and bake for 20 minutes or until a toothpick inserted comes out clean

Once the sponge is done, let it cool. Now, make your frosting (I'm partial towards the ganache)

Slice the cake in half with a serrated knife. Spread the frosting on one layer and sandwich with the other

Cover the cake with the rest of the frosting and let it set in the fridge for a few hours

MOLTEN CHOCOLATE CAKE

Makes 4 medium-sized ramekins

This recipe is adapted from my friend Marie's recipe. Her grandmother used to make this cake for her when she was little and Marie often made it for me when I was craving chocolate or feeling blue. It is an extremely easy recipe that can be whipped up in 5 minutes. I suggest using good quality chocolate since it is the star ingredient. This cake is best baked right before serving. You can make the batter and refrigerate it for a few hours, but always bake it just before you want to serve it.

200g dark chocolate
200g butter
150g castor sugar
4 eggs
60g flour

Melt the chocolate and butter over a hot water bath or in the microwave

Add the castor sugar and wait for the mixture to cool

Once cool, add the eggs, one by one, whisking well after each addition

Fold in the flour and pour the batter into the ramekins

Bake at 200C for 7–8 minutes. The edges should be cooked while the centre should remain wobbly

Baked cheesecake, page 63

Chocolate chip muffins, page 84

Blueberry muffins, page 83

Carrot cake, page 68

Red velvet brownies, page 50

Mango cheesecake, page 64

TEA TIME

MUFFINS

LOAF CAKES

MUFFINS

I love cupcakes, I like muffins. The only reason I love them less than cupcakes is the absence of frosting, which is my favourite part of a cupcake.

But more technically, the difference between muffins and cupcakes is in the way they are both made. For muffins, we mix the dry ingredients and wet ingredients separately and then combine the two, and so the final texture of a muffin varies from that of a cupcake. While a cupcake is rich, dense and crumbly, a muffin is more bread like, which allows it to be sliced up and toasted.

BLUEBERRY MUFFINS

Makes 8 muffins

I know I said muffins come second in my list, but blueberry muffins spread with a dollop of butter and jam can really make for a good start to my day. If you have access to fresh blueberries then you can replace the jam with them.

150g flour	Whisk together the oil, milk, egg and vanilla till combined
200g castor sugar	
½tsp salt	In a separate bowl, sift together flour, sugar, salt and baking powder
2tsp baking powder	
80ml vegetable oil	Add the dry ingredients to the wet and mix well
1 large egg	
100ml milk	Add blueberry jam and fold with a spatula
1 ½tsp vanilla essence	
150g blueberry jam/preserve	Fill the muffin liners halfway
	Bake at 165C for 20 minutes or till a skewer inserted comes out clean

CHOCOLATE CHIP MUFFINS

Makes around 10 muffins

A fresh, warm chocolate chip muffin smeared with chocolate sauce is excellent as a decadent weekend breakfast or a snack on a rushed day.

200g flour
150g castor sugar
30g cocoa powder
2tsp baking soda
175g chocolate chips
2 eggs
100ml vegetable oil
200g curd/yogurt
50ml water

Whisk together the vegetable oil, eggs and castor sugar till combined

In a separate bowl, sift together the flour, cocoa powder and baking soda

Add the eggs and oil to the flour and whisk till combined

Add the curd to the water and whisk. Fold into the batter

Add 125g chocolate chips and mix into the batter.
Fill the muffin liners halfway

Sprinkle the remaining chocolate chips on each muffin

Bake at 165C for 20 minutes or till a skewer inserted comes out clean

LOAF CAKES

There is an English bakery in Paris that I often visited for cake and tea. Nobody does that better than the British, right? At the bakery I was always greeted with an array of freshly baked loaves of cake on a large table. I would slice my favourites, and take them to my usual corner table to enjoy with a cup of the fragrant English Breakfast tea. While I was writing the recipes for this section I found myself thinking of the bakery with a smile on my face. These cakes are best served warm and straight out of the oven. However, you can store them in an airtight container for 4–5 days.

ALMOND CHOCOLATE CHIP LOAF

This is a combination that I adore. The almond powder makes the cake moist and gives it a fuller texture. I've used dark chocolate but you could use milk or white chocolate as well. Another good addition to this cake is butterscotch chips.

150g butter

85g powdered brown sugar

2 eggs

150g flour

1tsp baking powder

50g almond powder

125g chocolate chips

50g almond flakes for garnishing

Whisk together butter and powdered brown sugar till light and fluffy

Add eggs and whisk till properly combined

Sift flour and baking powder in a separate bowl

Fold in the flour and almond powder with a spatula

Add the chocolate chips and mix

Pour into a 300g lined loaf tin, garnish with the almond flakes and bake at 165C for 20–25 minutes or untill a skewer inserted in the centre comes out clean

BANANA WALNUT LOAF

This is my feel-good cake. Every time I'm stressed or want to take my mind off something, I make a loaf of banana walnut cake. It's best eaten warm with a small cup of hot chocolate.

....

3 eggs

150g butter

225g brown sugar

1tsp vanilla essence

225g flour

1½tsp baking powder

3 bananas, mashed

150g roasted walnuts, chopped

1tsp cinnamon powder

Whisk together the butter, brown sugar and vanilla essence till thick

Add eggs one at a time, whisking well after each addition

Mix in the mashed bananas and cinnamon powder

Sift together the flour and baking powder and fold it into the batter

Add the chopped roasted walnuts and mix

Pour into a lined 300g loaf tin and bake at 165C for 20–25 minutes

LEMON AND ALMOND LOAF

My chef in Paris used to love this cake and often made us whip it up in time for our coffee break. The almonds make the cake slightly dense but also help keep it moist.

125g butter
125g castor sugar
2 eggs
100g flour
1tsp baking soda
50g ground almonds
1tsp lemon zest
5tsp lemon juice

Whisk the butter and castor sugar together till thick

Add the eggs one at a time and whisk well till combined

Sift the flour and baking soda together and add to the mixture

Add the ground almonds, lemon zest and lemon juice and give it a final mix

Bake in a lined 250g loaf tin at 165C for 20 minutes

DENSE CHOCOLATE LOAF

This is an all-time favourite in my kitchen. My team loves making and eating it. This cake travels very well and I often make it when I have to send yummy gifts to friends and family living in other cities. You could add some nuts to this cake to give it texture or toss some chocolate chips on top to dress it up a little.

100g butter
80g dark chocolate
125g castor sugar
100g water
70g flour
5g cocoa powder
1 egg
½tsp baking powder

Over a double boiler, melt together the butter, dark chocolate, castor sugar and water

Once cooled properly, add the egg and mix

Sift together the flour and baking powder and fold into the chocolate mix with a spatula till mixed

Pour into a lined 300g loaf tin and bake at 180C for 15–18 minutes

BANANA CHOCOLATE CHIP LOAF

Bananas are my comfort fruit. Since bananas are available all through the year this recipe is very convenient. The chocolate chips add a little twist to the traditional banana bread. You could add powdered cinnamon to this recipe too.

180g flour
150g castor sugar
½tsp salt
2tsp baking powder
80ml vegetable oil
1 large egg
80ml milk
1½tsp vanilla essence
3 bananas, mashed
120gm chocolate chips

In a bowl, sift together flour, castor sugar, salt and baking powder

In a separate bowl, whisk together vegetable oil, milk, egg and vanilla essence

Add the dry ingredients to the wet and mix properly with a spatula

Add the mashed bananas and the chocolate chips and mix

Pour into a lined 300g loaf tin and bake at 165C for 20–25 minutes or until a skewer, when inserted in the centre of the cake, comes out clean

VANILLA BEAN LOAF (EGGLESS)

Vanilla is the most beautiful but the most underrated flavour.
I truly enjoy vanilla in my desserts and try and use it in as many
recipes as I can. This is a simple no-fuss recipe. If you have
access to vanilla beans, please use them. If not, the extract
or essence will do.

200g condensed milk
125ml milk
100g butter
15g castor sugar
125g flour
½tsp baking soda
1tsp baking powder
½ vanilla bean or
2tsp vanilla essence or extract

Whisk together butter and castor sugar till light and fluffy

Split the vanilla bean, scrape out the seeds and add to the mixture
and mix well. If using essence or extract, add now

Add the milk and condensed milk and whisk till mixed well

Sift together the flour, baking soda and baking powder and fold into
the above mix with a spatula

Bake at 180C for 20–22 minutes in a lined 300g loaf tin or until a
skewer, when inserted in the centre of the cake, comes out clean

COFFEE WALNUT LOAF

2tsp coffee powder

2tsp hot water

200g butter

200g brown sugar

3 eggs

1tsp baking powder

175g flour

150g walnuts, chopped

Dissolve the coffee powder in the hot water

Whisk together the butter, brown sugar and coffee till light and fluffy

Add in the eggs and beat till mixed well

Sift together the flour and baking powder and fold into the above mixture

Add the chopped walnuts and mix into the batter

Pour into a lined 300g loaf tin

Preheat the oven to 175C and bake for 30 minutes or till a skewer inserted comes out clean

Chocolate tartlets, page 113

Pumpkin tart, page 109

Strawberry tart, page 111

Mango tartlets, page 120

Lemon meringue tart, page 110

TARTS

TARTLETS

When I moved back to Mumbai, the hardest thing to do in the kitchen was to roll out tart dough on a hot humid day (which is almost every single day!). The butter starts to melt and the dough becomes sticky making it impossible to roll it out. Over time my friend Daniel and I worked out a recipe which is perfect for this weather. The thing to remember while making tart dough is that it is not instant—it requires time and patience. But the good thing is you can make plenty at once and stock it in the freezer for up to a month. And then each time you get a lemon tart craving, cut out a piece of dough, let it come to room temperature, and roll away!

SOME THINGS TO KEEP IN MIND WHILE MAKING TARTS

Always start with cold butter

Use your hands to rub the butter and flour together. This helps to coat the flour properly and will give you a flaky crust.

Don't overwork the dough. Your dough should hold together but should not be wet.

Once the dough is ready, wrap it with cling film and put it back in the fridge for about an hour so it has rested, allowing the moisture to be evenly distributed.

Always roll the dough out on a lightly floured surface or between 2 baking sheets.

Once you've lined the tart ring, put it back in the refrigerator for a few minutes before baking.

LINING A TART RING

See step-by-step with pictures on pages 116–117

BAKING BLIND

Line the tart ring with the dough and then with a fork, make a few marks. This ensures that the base of the tart does not rise. Then place parchment paper or butter paper inside the shell and fill with a layer of beans (rajma, chana etc.). The beans help weigh the pastry down and prevent it from rising unevenly. Bake at 175C for approximately 12 minutes or till the pastry has browned slightly and the tart begins to leave the edges of the ring. Take it out of the oven, remove the beans and then continue baking for another 5–7 minutes so that the bottom of the tart is cooked. Remove and set it aside to cool.

HALF BAKING

Line the tart ring with the dough and then with a fork, make a few marks. This ensures that the base of the tart does not rise. Bake the tart at 175C for 10 minutes or till the pastry gets a slight colour to it. Take it out of the oven and set aside to cool.

CHOCOLATE TART DOUGH

Makes 2 (7-inch) tarts

....

1 egg

150g icing sugar

200g flour

50g cocoa powder

125g cold butter
cut into 1-inch cubes

Whisk together the egg and icing sugar till light and fluffy

Sift the flour and cocoa powder and add to the above mixture

Add the cold butter cubes and use your fingers to crumble the mixture together. Using your palms, knead the dough till it comes together

Cling wrap and refrigerate for a minimum of 2 hours before using

BASIC TART DOUGH

Makes 2 (7-inch) tarts

300g flour

200g cold butter cut into
1-inch cubes

100g icing sugar

1 egg

1 tsp vanilla essence

Crack an egg into a small bowl and beat it. Set it aside

Sift the flour and icing sugar through a large sieve in a large bowl. This will aerate the dough and help make the finished tart crisp and light

Rub the cold butter cubes into the flour with your fingers until the mixture is even coloured and resembles fine breadcrumbs

Make a well in the centre and then pour in the beaten egg and vanilla essence

Lightly knead until the dough comes together

Put it on a work surface and shape it into a rough ball. Do not overwork the dough or the pastry will be tough

Cling wrap and refrigerate for a minimum of 2 hours

APPLE TART

Makes 1 (7-inch) tart

This tart uses 2 layers of apples. First, there's a layer of puréed apples in the base and then a second layer of sliced apples is arranged prettily on top. I recommend using Granny Smith apples or any firm type of apple (Golden Delicious is a great substitute). Once you cut the apples you can put them in a bowl of cold water so they don't start to brown. This tart is best eaten warm, with either fresh whipped cream or vanilla ice cream.

One 7-inch tart ring lined with pastry dough, half-baked, *recipe (page 106), technique (page 104)*

BOTTOM LAYER
2 Granny Smith apples
30g butter
30g castor sugar
50ml water
1 tsp cinnamon powder

TOP LAYER
3 Granny Smith apples
30g butter
30g brown sugar

Peel, core and halve all the apples. Place them cut-side down and cut them into 2 mm slices

Cook the slices of 2 apples in a saucepan with water, butter and cinnamon powder

Once the apples are tender, use the back of the spoon to mash them and make a purée

In a half-baked tart, use a spoon to spread the purée evenly across the base

Arrange the remaining sliced apples on top so that the edges overlap and they form a circle. Then arrange another circle inside, filling the centre with chopped apples

Melt the butter and brush it on the apples. Sprinkle the brown sugar on top

Bake at 180C till the apples start to brown

APRICOT TART

Makes 2 (7-inch) free-fold tarts

....

TART

Basic Tart Dough (page 106)

ALMOND CREAM

100g butter, soft
100g castor sugar
100g almond powder
2 eggs
10g flour

FILLING

1 tin of canned apricots (400g)

Preheat the oven to 180C

In a medium-sized bowl, mix together the butter, castor sugar and almond powder till evenly blended

Add eggs and mix thoroughly. Fold in the flour

Roll out the tart dough till 9 or 10-inch wide and ½-inch thick and place on a sheet of butter paper

Spread the almond cream evenly across the surface of the tart leaving 2 inches at the edges

Place the apricots on top and then fold in the uncoated edges of the dough over the filling, forming pleats. Place this in a baking tray

Bake for 30 minutes or till the cream turns golden brown

PUMPKIN TART

Makes 1 (7-inch) tart

I came to this recipe very serendipitously. A customer rang me a couple of years ago and asked for a pumpkin tart for Thanksgiving. I'd never made it before but I love challenges, so after three trial runs, I found a recipe that worked for me. It was a big hit and remains one of my favourite stories to tell.

One 7-inch tart ring lined with pastry dough, half baked (page 104)

100g brown sugar
110g castor sugar
2tsp cinnamon powder
½tsp salt
¼tsp nutmeg powder
½tsp ground ginger
¼tsp ground cloves
400g pumpkin purée
30ml vegetable oil
2 eggs
1tsp vanilla essence
300ml milk

Stir together the brown sugar, castor sugar, cinnamon powder, salt, nutmeg powder, ground ginger and ground cloves and set aside

Whisk together the pumpkin purée, vegetable oil, eggs, vanilla essence and milk in a separate bowl till evenly blended

Add the spices to this mixture

Pour into the prepared half-baked tart and bake in a 200C preheated oven for around 45 minutes or till a skewer inserted in the middle of the tart comes out clean

The centre may be a little wobbly but it will firm up outside the oven while it is cooling

LEMON MERINGUE TART

Makes 1 (7-inch) tart

One of the few times I am happy to eat a dessert that doesn't have chocolate is when I make this lemon meringue tart. It is the perfect combination of sweet and tart. I learnt how to make this from a friend's mother in Paris. Most people use an Italian meringue (with sugar syrup) but she used a French meringue to top the lemon filling. French meringue is just egg whites whipped firm with castor sugar. This recipe calls for a blowtorch to caramelize the meringue. If you don't have one, simply put your finished tart in the oven and bake for an extra 5 minutes.

One 7-inch tart ring lined with pastry dough, half-baked (page 104)

FILLING
Juice of 3 lemons
165g castor sugar
40g butter
1 tsp lemon zest
4 eggs

MERINGUE TOPPING
60g egg whites
75g castor sugar

Mix the lemon juice, lemon zest and castor sugar in a saucepan

Add the eggs and stir till combined

Cook on low heat and keep stirring so that the eggs don't cook/scramble

Just before the mixture starts to boil, add the butter and cook till the colour of the mixture changes. It should turn a pale yellow

Take it off the heat and pour into the tart shell

Bake for 12–15 minutes at 130C. Let it cool

In a clean bowl, whisk the egg whites

When they start to froth, slowly start adding the sugar and whisk till stiff peaks are formed

Spread the meringue evenly on top of the lemon tart

Use a blowtorch to glaze the meringue

STRAWBERRY TART

Makes 1 (7-inch) tart

....

FOR THE SHELL

One (7-inch) blind baked tart
(page 104)
200g whipped cream, sweetened
250g strawberries, halved
10g icing sugar

Whip the cream in a stainless steel bowl until firm peaks are formed

Pour the whipped cream into the blind baked tart and spread evenly

Place the strawberries upside down on top of the cream and cover the entire surface of the tart

Set in the fridge for about 1 hour

Dust with icing sugar before serving

TARTLETS

I enjoy baking mini tarts for parties. They are easy to make and you can whip up a variety in no time. While planning a party or setting a dessert table, a platter of assorted tartlets looks fabulous while also working as a great conversation starter. These are some ideas of flavours that you can put together. Try to make an assortment of chocolate-based and fruit tarts—they give you a variety of colour, flavour and texture.

CHOCOLATE TARTLETS

Makes 12 tartlets

An all-time favourite, this sinful chocolate tartlet will definitely hit the spot for all chocolate lovers.

12 blind baked chocolate tartlets *(recipe on page 105 and technique on page 104)*

150g chocolate ganache (You can use any truffle recipe as a filling!)

Pour chocolate ganache into a blind baked tartlet and fill till the brim

Set for an hour in the fridge

Top it with some of your favourite nuts or just have it as is

CHOCOLATE BANANA TARTLETS

Makes 12 tartlets

The buttery tart base, chopped bananas and a silky chocolate ganache come together deliciously well. I prefer using dark chocolate but milk chocolate also works.

12 blind baked tartlets
(recipe on page 106 and technique on page 104)
120g chocolate ganache
5 bananas, chopped

Start by filling half the tart with chopped bananas and then top it with your choice of ganache

Refrigerate for a minimum of 1 hour before serving

You could use chopped pears or strawberries instead of bananas

Wasabi cupcakes, page 144

Rose cupcake, page 126

Roll out the tart dough till it is 0.5 thick

Use your thumb to press the dough down and line the tart

With the help of your rolling pin transfer the dough onto the tart ring

To blind bake a tart, fill with any beans

Oreo cupcakes, page 140

Vanilla cupcake, page 125

DOUBLE CHOCOLATE TARTLETS

Makes 12

12 blind baked tartlets
*(recipe on page 106 and
technique on page 104)*

100g white chocolate ganache
(page 154)

100g dark chocolate ganache

Fill half the tart with dark chocolate ganache

After you have refrigerated it for a minimum of 30 minutes,
pour in the white chocolate ganache

Set it in the refrigerator

MANGO TARTLETS

Makes 12 tartlets

A great way to use up mangoes in summer. Use whichever kind of mango you find locally. In fact you can use ANY fruit of your choice instead of mangoes—strawberries, kiwis, oranges, blueberries, etc.

12 blind baked tartlets (recipe on page 106 and technique on page 104)

150g whipped cream

2 medium-sized mangoes

Peel and chop one mango. Slice the other one and keep it aside to decorate the tart

Place the chopped mangoes at the base of the tart

Cover the mangoes with whipped cream and refrigerate for a minimum of 30 minutes before serving

CUPCAKES

I love baking cupcakes like I love dancing. Both give me immense joy and bring out the best in me. What I love the most about baking cupcakes is how creative you can get with the recipes. I have selected the recipes in this section to demonstrate to you a variety of baking methods. Once you find a recipe that you are comfortable with and enjoy baking, I encourage you to experiment with the flavours. It could be as simple as adding cinnamon to a frosting or mixing and matching unexpected base recipes together with a frosting recipe. Did I mention how cupcake baking can liven up any children's party?

All these recipes can be adapted to make full cakes too. Instead of piping the batter into a cupcake tray, just use a cake tin, and voila! You have a cake base ready.

Play, have fun and enjoy yourself. Just like on the dance floor.

VANILLA CUPCAKES

Makes approximately 24 mini cupcakes

This classic is extremely versatile—bake in a cake mould to get a sponge cake instead! You can play around with the colours of the frosting.   Involve your kids in decorating the cupcakes.

110g butter
200g castor sugar
1tsp vanilla essence
2 eggs
150g flour
1tsp baking powder
80ml milk

(Vanilla buttercream frosting on page 153)

Preheat the oven to 175C

In a bowl, beat the butter, castor sugar and vanilla essence till light and fluffy

Add the eggs one at a time, whisking after each addition until mixed well

Sift together the flour and baking powder

Add the milk and mix with a spatula. Then fold in the flour

Line a cupcake mould with liners and pipe the batter into cupcake liners till ¾ full

Bake for 15 minutes or till a skewer, when inserted in the centre of the cake, comes out clean

ROSE CUPCAKES

Makes approximately 24 mini cupcakes

A lot of Indian desserts have a strong rose flavour, so I wanted to make something with it. This recipe is dedicated to all of us who love Roohafza.

110g butter

200g castor sugar

1tsp rose essence

2 eggs

150g flour

1tsp baking powder

80ml milk

(Rose cream cheese frosting on page 154)

In a bowl, beat the butter, castor sugar and rose essence till light and fluffy

Add the eggs one at a time, whisking after each addition until mixed well

Sift together the flour and baking powder

Add the milk and mix with a spatula. Then fold in the flour

Line a cupcake mould with liners and pipe the batter into cupcake liners till ¾ full

Bake at 175C for 15 minutes or till a skewer, when inserted in the centre of the cake, comes out clean

CHOCOLATE CUPCAKES

Makes 20 mini cupcakes

Chocolate + Cupcake = happiness. Need I say more?!

....

100g butter

100g brown sugar

2 eggs

80g flour

25g cocoa powder

1tsp baking powder

40ml milk

(Chocolate ganache frosting on page 159)

In a bowl, whisk together the butter and brown sugar till light and fluffy

Add the eggs to the mixture and whisk till combined

Add the milk and mix thoroughly

Sift together the flour, cocoa powder and baking powder and fold into the mixture with a spatula

Line a cupcake mould with liners and scoop the batter into each liner till ¾ full

Bake at 175C for 15 minutes or till a skewer, when inserted in the centre of the cake, comes out clean.

PEANUT BUTTER CUPCAKES

Makes 24 mini cupcakes

These cupcakes are perfect for those who don't like their dessert too sweet. The peanut butter helps balance out the sweetness in the frosting. I've paired this cupcake with a buttercream frosting but you could match it with a chocolate ganache.

100g butter
150g castor sugar
2 eggs
80ml milk
150g flour
1tsp baking powder
50g chunky peanut butter

(Peanut butter buttercream frosting on page 160)

Whisk together the butter, peanut butter and castor sugar till light and fluffy

Add the eggs one at a time and beat till combined

Add the milk and mix well

Sift together flour and baking powder and fold into the mixture with a spatula

Line a cupcake mould with liners and pipe the batter into the cupcake liners till ¾ full

Bake at 175C for 15 minutes or till a skewer when inserted in the centre of the cake comes out clean

LEMON CUPCAKES

Makes approximately 24 mini cupcakes

These cupcakes are light, refreshing and perfect for a hot summer day. You could replace the lemon with orange. I like using a cream cheese frosting for this cupcake but you could use buttercream too.

110g butter	In a bowl, beat the butter, castor sugar, lemon zest and lemon juice till light and fluffy
200g castor sugar	
1tsp lemon zest	
1tsp lemon juice	Add the eggs one at a time, whisking after each addition until mixed well
2 eggs	
1tsp baking powder	Sift together the flour and baking powder
150g flour	
80ml milk	Add the milk and mix with a spatula. Then fold in the flour
(Lemon cream cheese frosting on page 162)	Line a cupcake mould with liners and pipe the batter into cupcake liners till ¾ full
	Bake at 175C for 15 minutes or till a skewer when inserted in the centre of the cake comes out clean

MOCHA CUPCAKES

Makes 20 mini cupcakes

I function much better once I've had my daily dose of caffeine. The idea of these cupcakes came about when I decided to mix chocolate with coffee. Two cravings, one solution!

100g butter
100g brown sugar
2 eggs
80g flour
1tsp baking powder
25g cocoa powder
40ml milk
2tsp instant coffee
2tsp hot water

(Chocolate ganache frosting on page 159)

Dissolve the instant coffee in the hot water and set aside

In a bowl, whisk together the butter and brown sugar till light and fluffy

Add the eggs to the mixture and whisk till combined

Add the milk and instant coffee dissolved in water and mix thoroughly

Sift together the flour, cocoa powder and baking powder and fold into the mixture with a spatula

Line a cupcake mould with liners and scoop the batter into each liner till ⅔ full

Bake at 175C for 15 minutes or till a skewer, when inserted in the centre of the cake, comes out clean

MINT CHOCOLATE CUPCAKES

Makes 24 mini cupcakes

The chocolate base is very dense but has a subtle taste of mint, and a cooling buttercream icing. You can look at this as the perfect palette cleanser, to prepare you for the rest of the flavours!

....

200g dark chocolate
200g butter
150g castor sugar
4 eggs
3tsp mint essence
60g flour

(Mint buttercream frosting on page 161)

Melt the butter and dark chocolate in a microwave

Once cool, add the castor sugar and whisk till mixed together

Add the eggs and mint essence to the mixture and whisk well

Fold in the flour with a spatula

Line a cupcake mould with liners and pipe the batter into cupcake liners till ¾ full

Bake at 175C for 15 minutes or till a skewer when inserted in the centre of the cake comes out clean

CHAI CUPCAKES

Makes 24 mini cupcakes

I love thinking of ideas that incorporate everyday flavours in a dessert. It brings in a surprise element, yet the taste is familiar and comforting.

110g butter
200g castor sugar
1 tsp vanilla essence
2 eggs
1 tsp baking powder
150g flour
80ml chai
(made with milk and without sugar)

(Chai buttercream frosting on page 163)

In a bowl, beat the butter, castor sugar and vanilla essence till light and fluffy

Add the eggs one at a time, whisking after each addition till mixed well

Sift together the flour and baking powder

Add the chai and mix with a spatula. Then fold in the flour

Line a cupcake mould with liners and pipe the batter into cupcake liners till ¾ full

Bake at 175C for 15 minutes or till a skewer, when inserted in the centre of the cake, comes out clean

CINNAMON SPICE CUPCAKES

Makes 24 mini cupcakes

These cupcakes remind me of Christmas markets in Paris. Mulled wine, sold at these markets, is the inspiration for this cupcake.

....

110g butter

200g castor sugar

2 eggs

1tsp cinnamon powder

½tsp grated ginger

A pinch of cardamom powder

150g flour

1tsp baking powder

80ml milk

(Cinnamon spice buttercream frosting on page 164)

In a bowl, beat the butter and castor sugar till light and fluffy

Add the cinnamon powder, ginger and cardamom powder and mix

Add the eggs one at a time, whisking after each addition until mixed well

Sift together the flour and baking powder

Now, to the above mixture add the milk and mix with a spatula. Then fold in the flour

Line a cupcake mould with liners and pipe the batter into cupcake liners till ¾ full

Bake at 175C for 15 minutes or till a skewer when inserted in the centre of the cake comes out clean

OAT CRUMBLE CUPCAKES

Makes 20 mini cupcakes

This cupcake is perfect to carry along for picnics or long car drives. It doesn't have frosting so it travels very well. The oat crumble adds a wonderful crunch and texture to the cake base.

CRUMBLE
100g butter
100g brown sugar
120g oats
1tbsp honey

For the crumble, heat the butter, brown sugar, oats and honey in a saucepan till it reaches a liquid consistency and set aside to cool

In a bowl, whisk the butter and castor sugar till light and fluffy

CUPCAKE
100g butter
100g castor sugar
1 egg
80g flour

Add the egg and whisk

Add the flour and fold into the mixture

Line a cupcake mould with liners and pipe the cupcake batter till each liner is half full

Taking a small portion of the crumble, flatten it with your fingers and top each cupcake with it

Bake at 175C for 15 minutes or till a skewer when inserted in the centre of the cake comes out clean

Lemon cupcakes, page 129

Chocolate cupcakes, page 127

Red velvet cupcake, page 141

Chai cupcakes, page 132

CHOCOLATE PEAR CUPCAKES

Makes 15 mini cupcakes

The pears add moisture to this cake and so this is another cupcake that doesn't require frosting. Pears and chocolate is a unique combination and works very well together.

100g butter
100g brown sugar
1 tsp cinnamon powder
2 eggs
80g flour
25g cocoa powder
1 tsp baking powder
30ml pear syrup (from the can)
1 whole pear (canned)

In a bowl, whisk together the butter, brown sugar and cinnamon powder till light and fluffy

Add the eggs and whisk till combined

Sift together the flour, cocoa powder and baking powder and fold into the mixture with a spatula

Add the pear syrup and mix

Line a cupcake mould with liners and scoop the batter into each liner till ⅔ full

Cut the pear into small, thin slices and place on top of each cupcake

Bake at 175C for 15 minutes or till a skewer when inserted in the centre of the cake comes out clean

OREO CUPCAKES

Makes 20 mini cupcakes

The sweet frosting and moist cake makes this one very popular with children. The recipe uses the biscuit in the cake base and the filling in the frosting.

100g butter

100g brown sugar

2 eggs

80g flour

15g cocoa powder

1 tsp baking powder

40ml milk

6 Oreo cookies, cream separated and reserved

(Oreo cream cheese frosting on page 165)

In a bowl, whisk together the butter and brown sugar till light and fluffy

Add the eggs and whisk till combined

Add the milk and mix thoroughly

Sift together the flour, cocoa powder and baking powder and fold into the mixture with a spatula

Crush the Oreo cookies till fine crumbs are formed and add 30g of the crumbs to the above mixture. Mix thoroughly. Set aside the extra crumbs

Line a cupcake mould with liners and scoop the batter into each liner till ⅔ full

Bake at 175C for 15 minutes or till a skewer when inserted in the centre of the cake comes out clean

RED VELVET CUPCAKES

Makes 24 mini cupcakes

This is the most popular cupcake we make at Le15. We can stock all our refrigerators with only the red velvet cupcakes and they will all get sold in an hour. I love the combination of the slightly acidic cake base and a sweet cream cheese frosting. The deep berry colour of the cupcake base makes it very attractive and I would recommend using a liquid food colouring rather than a gel colour. If you prefer to skip the food colour, you could use beetroot juice instead but this will affect the flavour, and the colour of your cake will vary.

55g butter
150g castor sugar
1 egg
1 tbsp red food colouring
1 tbsp unsweetened cocoa
½tsp vanilla essence
100g yogurt
A pinch of salt
120g flour
½tsp cider vinegar
½tsp baking soda

(Cream cheese frosting on page 148)

Preheat oven to 180C

In a large bowl, on the medium speed of an electric mixer, cream the butter and castor sugar till light and fluffy, for about 5 minutes. Add the egg

In a small bowl, whisk together the red food colouring, cocoa and vanilla essence. Add to the batter and beat well

In a measuring cup, stir the salt into the yogurt and give a slight whisk. Add to the batter. Now add the flour

In a small bowl, stir together the cider vinegar and baking soda. Add to the batter and mix well. Using a rubber spatula, scrape down the batter in the bowl, making sure the ingredients are well blended and the batter is smooth

Line a cupcake mould with liners and pipe the batter into the cupcake liners till ¾ full

Bake each tray for 20 minutes, or till a skewer inserted in the centre of the cake comes out clean

SAFFRON PISTACHIO CUPCAKES

Makes approximately 24 mini cupcakes

As much as I love receiving chocolates and cakes for Diwali, I have a soft spot for the little kesar pista barfi that my father usually buys from a shop close to home. This recipe is inspired by that saffron pistachio mithai, which with its festive Indian touch makes for a perfect Diwali gift.

Few strands of saffron

80ml milk

110g butter

200g castor sugar

1tsp vanilla essence

2 eggs

150g flour

1tsp baking powder

(Saffron pistachio buttercream frosting on page 167)

Dissolve the saffron strands in the milk

In a bowl, beat the butter, castor sugar and vanilla essence till light and fluffy

Add the eggs one at a time, whisking after each addition until mixed well

Sift together the flour and baking powder

Add the saffron milk and mix with a spatula. Then fold in the flour

Line a cupcake mould with liners and pipe the batter into the liners till ¾ full

Bake at 175C for 15 minutes or till a skewer, when inserted in the centre of the cake, comes out clean

EGGLESS CHOCOLATE CUPCAKES

Makes 24 mini cupcakes

When I was studying in Paris I remember asking my chef at school how to make an eggless cupcake. He seemed baffled. The idea of not using eggs in a cake recipe was just not acceptable to him. I explained to him that eggs are a big concern in India and then gave him this recipe that my mother usually used when baking eggless cupcakes.

100g butter
15g castor sugar
125ml milk
200g condensed milk
150g melted dark chocolate
125g flour
½tsp baking soda
1tsp baking powder

(Chocolate ganache frosting on page 159)

Whisk together butter and castor sugar till light and fluffy

Add the milk and condensed milk and mix well

Add the melted dark chocolate and whisk

Sift together the flour, baking soda and baking powder and fold into the mixture with a spatula

Line a cupcake mould with liners and scoop the batter into each liner till ⅔ full

Bake at 175C for 15 minutes or till a skewer when inserted in the centre of the cake comes out clean

WASABI CUPCAKES

Makes approximately 24 mini cupcakes

One of my favourite pastry shops in Paris is run by a Japanese chef. All of his desserts are influenced by his culture. The wasabi cupcake is dedicated to him and all the times I have lined up outside his store waiting to get my hands on a matcha millefeuille.

110g butter
200g castor sugar
1 tsp vanilla essence
2 eggs
150g flour
1 tsp baking powder
80ml milk
5–7g wasabi paste

(Wasabi buttercream frosting on page 168)

In a bowl, beat the butter, castor sugar, wasabi paste and vanilla essence
till light and fluffy

Add the eggs one at a time, whisking after each addition till mixed well

Sift together the flour and baking powder

Add the milk and mix with a spatula. Then fold in the flour

Line a cupcake mould with liners and pipe the batter into the liners till ¾ full

Bake at 175C for 15 minutes or till a skewer, when inserted in the centre of the cake, comes out clean

HAZELNUT CHOCOLATE CHIP CUPCAKES

Makes 24 mini cupcakes

....

100g butter

In a bowl, whisk together the butter and brown sugar till light and fluffy

100g brown sugar

2 eggs

Add the eggs and whisk till combined. Be careful not to over-whisk

40g flour

40g hazelnut powder
(first roasted and then powdered)

Sift together the flour, hazelnut powder and baking powder and fold into the above mixture

1tsp baking powder

40ml milk

Add the milk and stir to combine

100g chocolate chips
(tossed in a bit of flour)

Mix the chocolate chips into the batter and give it a gentle stir

Line a cupcake mould with liners and scoop the batter into each liner till ⅔ full

Bake at 175C for 15 minutes or till a skewer, when inserted in the centre of the cake, comes out clean

NUTELLA CUPCAKES

Makes 20 mini cupcakes

I'm amazed at the number of Nutella jars we go through each day in our kitchen. I ask my team to hide Nutella from me otherwise I'll be seen grabbing a spoon and eating Nutella straight from the jar (the best way to do it!).

100g butter
100g brown sugar
2 eggs
80g flour
25g cocoa powder
1tsp baking powder
40ml milk
100g soft Nutella

(Nutella buttercream frosting on page 166)

In a bowl, whisk together the butter and brown sugar till the brown sugar specks start disappearing

Add the eggs and whisk till light and fluffy

Sift together the flour, cocoa powder and baking powder and fold into the above mixture with a spatula. Add the milk and mix thoroughly

Line a cupcake mould with liners and scoop the batter into each liner till ⅔ full

Bake at 175C for 15 minutes or till a skewer, when inserted in the centre of the cake, comes out clean

Once the cupcakes have cooled, make a hole in the middle of each cupcake with a knife and spoon in the Nutella

FROSTINGS

CREAM CHEESE FROSTING

125g cream cheese, cold
50g butter, at room temperature
1 tsp lemon zest
300g icing sugar, sifted

In a large bowl, beat the cream cheese and butter till smooth. Add the lemon zest and whisk well

Gradually add the icing sugar, 1 cup at a time, beating continuously until smooth and creamy

Cover and refrigerate the frosting for 2–3 hours before using

ROSE BUTTERCREAM FROSTING

100g butter
2tsp rose syrup
225g icing or powdered sugar
1 tbsp milk
1 tsp light pink food colour

In a bowl, whisk the butter till smooth. Add the rose syrup and whisk

Gradually add in the icing sugar and whisk till properly mixed

Add the milk and beat to combine. Keep beating till the frosting is light and fluffy. It will take around 5 minutes

Add the light pink food colour and mix till the colour is even

If not using right away, cover it with cling wrap to prevent it from drying

ROSE GANACHE FROSTING

200g white chocolate
150ml cream
1 tsp rose syrup
½tsp rose essence

Chop the chocolate and place in a medium-sized bowl

Heat the cream till it comes to a boil

Pour the cream over the chocolate and whisk till the chocolate dissolves

Add the rose syrup and essence and finish whisking

CHOCOLATE BUTTERCREAM FROSTING

100g butter
½tsp vanilla essence
225g icing or powdered sugar
20g cocoa powder
1 tbsp milk

In a bowl, whisk the butter until smooth. Add the vanilla essence and whisk

Sift the icing sugar and cocoa powder and gradually add to the butter mixture and whisk till properly mixed

Add the milk and beat to combine

Keep whisking till the frosting is light and fluffy. It will take around 5 minutes. If not using right away, cover it with cling wrap to prevent it from drying

WHITE CHOCOLATE
GANACHE FROSTING

200g white chocolate
150ml cream

Chop the chocolate and place in a medium-sized bowl

Heat the cream till it comes to a boil

Pour the cream over the chocolate and whisk till the chocolate dissolves

Cling wrap and refrigerate if not using right away

VANILLA BUTTERCREAM FROSTING

100g butter
1 tsp vanilla essence
225g icing or powdered sugar
1 tbsp milk
A few drops of liquid food colouring
of your choice

In a bowl, whisk together the butter and vanilla essence until smooth

Gradually add in the icing sugar and whisk till mixed

Add the milk and beat to combine

Keep whisking till the frosting is light and fluffy. It should take you around 5 minutes if using a hand whisk

Add the food colour and mix till the colour is even

If not using right away, cover it with cling wrap and refrigerate to prevent it from drying

ROSE CREAM CHEESE FROSTING

125g cream cheese, cold
50g butter, at room temperature
2tsp rose syrup
300g icing sugar, sifted
1tsp light pink food colour

In a large bowl, whisk the cream cheese and butter until smooth. Add the rose syrup and beat well

Gradually add the icing sugar, whisking continuously until smooth and creamy

Add the light pink food colour and mix till the colour is even

Cover and refrigerate the frosting for 2–3 hours only

Classic chocolate mousse, page 194

Passion fruit pavlova, page 201

Chocolate chip pavlova, page 202

Strawberries and cream, page 200

CHOCOLATE GANACHE FROSTING

250g semi-sweet or bitter-sweet chocolate, cut into small pieces

180ml cream

20g butter

Place the chopped chocolate in a medium-sized stainless steel bowl and set aside

Heat the cream and butter in a saucepan over medium heat. Bring just to a boil

Immediately pour the boiling cream over the chocolate and allow it to stand for 5 minutes

Stir with a whisk until smooth

PEANUT BUTTER BUTTERCREAM FROSTING

100g butter
30g chunky peanut butter
225g icing or powdered sugar
1tbsp milk

In a bowl, whisk the butter till smooth. Add the peanut butter and whisk well

Gradually add in the icing sugar and milk and whisk till well-combined

Keep beating till the frosting is light and fluffy. If not using right away, cover it with cling wrap to prevent it from drying

MINT BUTTERCREAM FROSTING

100g butter
2tsp mint essence
225g icing or powdered sugar
1tbsp milk
1tsp green food colour

In a bowl, whisk the butter till smooth. Add the mint essence and whisk

Gradually add in the icing sugar and whisk till mixed

Add the milk and beat to combine. Keep beating till the frosting is light and fluffy. It will take around 5 minutes

Add the green food colour and mix till the colour is even

If not using right away, cover it with cling wrap and refrigerate to prevent it from drying

LEMON CREAM CHEESE FROSTING

125g cream cheese, cold
50g butter, at room temperature
2tsp lemon zest
300g icing sugar, sifted
1 tsp light yellow food colour

In a large bowl, whisk the cream cheese and butter till smooth.
Add the lemon zest and beat well

Gradually add the icing sugar, whisking continuously till smooth
and creamy

Add the light yellow food colour and mix till the colour is even

If not using right away, cover it with cling wrap to prevent
it from drying

CHAI BUTTERCREAM FROSTING

100g butter
¼tsp cardamom powder
½tsp cinnamon powder
¼tsp fresh grated ginger
225g icing or powdered sugar
1tbsp milk

In a bowl, whisk the butter till smooth. Add the cardamom powder, cinnamon powder, fresh grated ginger and whisk

Gradually add in the icing sugar and whisk till mixed

Add the milk and beat to combine. Keep beating till the frosting is light and fluffy. It will take around 5 minutes

If not using right away, cover it with cling wrap and refrigerate to prevent it from drying

CINNAMON SPICE BUTTERCREAM FROSTING

100g butter
¼th tsp cardamom powder
½tsp cinnamon powder
225g icing or powdered sugar
1 tbsp milk

In a bowl, whisk the butter till smooth. Add the cardamom powder and cinnamon powder and whisk

Gradually add in the icing sugar and whisk till mixed

Add the milk and beat to combine. Keep beating till the frosting is light and fluffy. It will take around 5 minutes

If not using right away, cover with cling wrap and refrigerate to prevent it from drying

OREO CREAM CHEESE FROSTING

125g cream cheese, cold
Cream of the Oreo cookies
50g butter, at room temperature
1 tsp vanilla essence
300g icing sugar, sifted
Reserved Oreo crumbs

In a large bowl, whisk the cream cheese, cream of the Oreo cookies and butter till smooth. Add the vanilla and beat well

Gradually add the icing sugar, whisking continuously till smooth and creamy and then add the reserved crumbs

If not using right away, cover with cling wrap and refrigerate to prevent it from drying

NUTELLA BUTTERCREAM FROSTING

100g butter
225g icing or powdered sugar
1 tbsp milk
30g Nutella

In a bowl, whisk the butter till smooth

Gradually add in the icing sugar and whisk till mixed

Add the milk and beat to combine

Add the Nutella and keep beating till the frosting is light and fluffy

If not using right away, cover it with cling wrap and refrigerate to prevent it from drying

SAFFRON PISTACHIO BUTTERCREAM FROSTING

1 tbsp milk
A few strands of saffron
100g butter
225g icing or powdered sugar
50g chopped pistachio for garnish

Soak the saffron strands in the milk and set aside

In a bowl, whisk the butter till smooth

Gradually add in the icing sugar and whisk till mixed

Add the saffron-infused milk and beat to combine. Keep beating till the frosting is light and fluffy. It will take around 5 minutes

If not using right away, cover it with cling wrap and refrigerate to prevent it from drying

WASABI BUTTERCREAM FROSTING

100g butter
225g icing or powdered sugar
1tbsp milk
1tsp wasabi paste
1tsp green food colour

In a bowl, whisk the butter and wasabi paste till smooth

Gradually add in the icing sugar and whisk till mixed

Add the milk and beat to combine. Keep beating till the frosting is light and fluffy. It will take around 5 minutes

Add the green food colour and mix till the colour is even

If not using right away, cover it with cling wrap to prevent it from drying

TRUFFLES

I was in complete awe when we made truffles in school the first time. I couldn't believe they were so simple, so flavourful and yet so versatile. A truffle, in essence, is just a hard ganache which is rolled into a ball and then dipped in chocolate or dusted with cocoa powder.

The best part about working in a chocolate shop in Paris was truffles. Making a ganache (chocolate + cream) is one of my favourite things. I love how boiled cream, when mixed with chocolate, just transforms into something so spectacular. I experiment with my ganache a lot. This is something I learnt when I was at the chocolate shop and has stayed with me till today. I look at ingredients and try new flavours and my mind starts working on how I can make a ganache with them. This section has some of my most loved flavour combinations like passion fruit and milk chocolate, green chilly or even wasabi-flavoured truffles.

All these recipes can be used as fillings for cakes, macarons or frostings for cupcakes.

RED VELVET TRUFFLES

Makes 16 truffles

Red velvet cake + truffle = delicious decadence. This has to be my favourite math equation. These truffles are a great option when you are baking cupcakes and have a few left over.

250g red velvet cake crumbs
75g Philadelphia Cream Cheese
180g white chocolate

Soften the cream cheese with a whisk and mix in 150g of the red velvet crumbs till thoroughly blended

Form small balls with the dough and refrigerate

Melt the white chocolate in a microwave

Drop the red velvet truffles in the chocolate and coat evenly

Scoop out the truffle with a fork so that the excess chocolate drips out and use a spoon to transfer it on to a wax paper to cool

While the chocolate is still soft, roll the truffles in the remaining 100g red velvet crumbs

Refrigerate for at least 20 minutes and then serve

Passion fruit truffles, page 183

Chocolate coconut truffles, page 189

Green chilly truffles, page 181

Milk chocolate and hazelnut truffles, page 182

Wasabi white chocolate truffles, page 186

Saffron pistachio truffles, page 185

Oreo cookie truffles, page 179

Dark chocolate and orange truffles, page 184

OREO COOKIE TRUFFLES (EGGLESS)

Makes 12 truffles

....

150g Oreo cookies
75g Philadelphia Cream Cheese
150g milk chocolate

Remove the cream from the Oreos and crush the cookies into fine crumbs. You can use a blender or a rolling pin. Set aside 2tbsp of the crumbs for later

Soften the cream cheese with a whisk

Add the Oreo crumbs and mix well

Now form small balls and refrigerate till hardened

In a microwave-safe bowl, melt the chocolate

Drop the Oreo cookie balls into the melted chocolate and coat evenly

Remove the truffle and leave on a wax paper to cool

While the truffles are still wet, roll them in the remaining Oreo crumbs

Refrigerate for a minimun of 20 minutes and then serve

WHITE CHOCOLATE AND
BAILEYS TRUFFLES (EGGLESS)

Makes 24 truffles

These delectable treats are the perfect dessert to make for a brunch. I always whip up a batch when friends come over.

250g white chocolate + 200g for coating

90ml cream

25ml Baileys

Melt 250g of the white chocolate and keep aside

Heat the cream in the microwave for 1½ minutes

Add the Baileys to the cream

Heat the cream again for 2 minutes

Add the Baileys cream mixture to the melted white chocolate and whisk till combined

Cool and refrigerate for at least 4 hours (up to overnight)

Make small balls and refrigerate them till hard

Melt the remaining white chocolate

Drop the balls into the melted white chocolate and coat evenly

Scoop out the truffles with a fork so that the excess white chocolate drips out and leave on a wax paper to cool

Refrigerate for at least an hour and then serve

GREEN CHILLY TRUFFLES (EGGLESS)
Makes 24 truffles

I work with a group of people that chow down chillies like it is the most natural thing to do. At lunch I'm used to seeing my team members bite into 3–4 green ones with every meal. Although I personally can't handle very hot food, my team inspired me to try adding chillies to dessert. I tried them with white chocolate and the result was spectacular. You feel the spice but the sweetness from the chocolate cuts it and this way even people like me can enjoy chillies!

250g white chocolate + 200g for coating
100ml cream
10g chopped green chillies

Melt 250g white chocolate and keep aside

Boil the cream on medium heat and add the chopped green chillies. Stir lightly and allow it to infuse for 5 minutes

Boil the cream again and then strain it over the white chocolate

Using a whisk, stir it gently till you get a homogenous mixture

Cool and refrigerate for at least 4 hours (up to overnight)

Make small balls and refrigerate till hardened

Melt the remaining white chocolate

Drop the balls into the melted chocolate and coat evenly

Scoop out the truffles with a fork so that the excess white chocolate drips out and leave on a wax paper to cool

Refrigerate for minimum 20 minutes and then serve

MILK CHOCOLATE AND HAZELNUT TRUFFLES (EGGLESS)

Makes 24 truffles

If you love hazelnuts then you will love this recipe. I'm sure you can tell by now that I have a great weakness for hazelnuts. Milk chocolate and hazelnuts make for a great combination but you could also use dark chocolate. If you have some hazelnut liqueur (frangelico) you could add a few drops right at the end for that extra kick.

300g milk chocolate
90ml cream
10g hazelnut powder
Finely chopped hazelnuts for coating

Melt the milk chocolate and set aside

Heat the cream for 2 minutes in a microwave or boil on medium heat

Add it to the melted milk chocolate and whisk till combined

Add the hazelnut powder and mix

Cool and refrigerate for at least 4 hours (up to overnight)

Make small balls and refrigerate till firm

Roll the truffles in the chopped hazelnuts until evenly coated

Refrigerate for 20 minutes and then serve

PASSION FRUIT TRUFFLES (EGGLESS)

Makes 24 truffles

Passion fruit and chocolate is one of my favourite flavour combinations. The light tartness of the fruit and the dense sweetness of the chocolate balance each other out well—the perfect marriage of flavours. If you like lemon as a flavour then you will enjoy this one. If you cannot find passion fruit, you can use any fruit purée—mango, strawberry, or even apple.

250g milk chocolate
60ml passion fruit purée
20ml cream
1tsp honey
20g butter
150g cocoa powder

Melt the milk chocolate and set aside

In a saucepan, boil the cream, passion fruit, butter and honey together

Pour over the melted milk chocolate and whisk till combined

Cool and refrigerate for at least 4 hours (up to overnight)

Make small balls and refrigerate till firm

Roll the hardened truffles in cocoa powder

Transfer the truffles to a sieve to dust off the excess cocoa powder

Refrigerate for 20 minutes and then serve

DARK CHOCOLATE AND
ORANGE TRUFFLES (EGGLESS)

Makes 24 truffles

250g dark chocolate
110ml cream
5–7g orange zest
Cocoa powder for rolling

Melt the dark chocolate and set aside

Heat the cream and orange zest in the microwave for 1½ minutes or boil over medium heat on the stove

Pour over the melted dark chocolate and whisk till combined

Cool and refrigerate for at least 4 hours (up to overnight)

Make small balls and refrigerate till firm

Roll them in cocoa powder till covered evenly

Transfer the truffles to a sieve to dust off the excess cocoa powder

Refrigerate again for 20 minutes and then serve

SAFFRON PISTACHIO TRUFFLES (EGGLESS)

Makes 24 truffles

....

250g white chocolate
90ml cream
A few strands of saffron
Finely chopped pistachio

Melt 250g white chocolate and set aside

Heat the cream and saffron in the microwave for 1 ½ minutes
or boil on a stove over medium heat

Pour over the melted chocolate and whisk till combined

Cool and refrigerate for at least 4 hours (up to overnight)

Make small balls and refrigerate till firm

Roll in the chopped pistachio till evenly coated

Refrigerate for 20 minutes and then serve

WASABI WHITE CHOCOLATE TRUFFLES (EGGLESS)

Makes 24 truffles

I use white chocolate with wasabi because I find the sweetness of the chocolate perfectly balances the pungent hit from the wasabi.

....

250g white chocolate
+ 200g for coating

90ml cream

5–7g wasabi paste

Melt 250g white chocolate and set aside

Heat the cream and wasabi paste in the microwave for 1½ minutes or boil over medium heat

Pour over the melted chocolate and whisk till combined

Cool and refrigerate for at least 4 hours (up to overnight)

Make small balls and refrigerate till hard

Melt the remaining white chocolate

Drop the balls into the melted chocolate and coat evenly

Scoop out the truffles with a fork so that the excess white chocolate drips out and leave on a wax paper to cool

Refrigerate for 20 minutes and then serve

ALMOND ROCKS (EGGLESS)

Makes around 35 rocks

I started using this recipe when I was 12. Every weekend I would make these chocolate almond rocks and take them to school with me on Monday to share with everyone. Obviously I was one of the most popular people in school.

Roasting the almonds enhances their flavour. You could substitute the almonds with any other nut or dry fruit. A combination of almond, cashew and butterscotch works very well with this recipe.

These treats are extremely easy to make and very addictive—beware!

200g whole roasted almonds
350g dark chocolate, melted
1 tsp orange zest

In a bowl, mix together the orange zest and the melted chocolate

Add the almonds and mix well

On silver foil, spoon out portions of the chocolate almond mix and refrigerate for around 45 minutes

Store in an airtight container in the fridge for up to a week

CHOCOLATE CORNFLAKES CLUSTERS (EGGLESS)

Makes around 15 clusters

A lazy cook's recipe—you don't even need an oven to make them. You could also make these in advance and store for a few days in the fridge. Make sure you toast the cornflakes in a pan before using and later store in an airtight container so that the cornflakes remain crisp. You could add more texture to these clusters by adding chopped dried apricots, butterscotch chips, chocolate chips or even desiccated coconut.

50g roasted cornflakes
250g dark chocolate, melted

Toast the cornflakes on a pan and let them cool

In a bowl, mix together the cornflakes and melted chocolate

On silver foil, spoon out portions of the chocolate cornflake mix and refrigerate for around 45 minutes

CHOCOLATE COCONUT
TRUFFLES (EGGLESS)
Makes 30 truffles

100ml coconut milk
50ml cream
350g dark chocolate
100g desiccated coconut

Melt the dark chocolate in the microwave or over a hot water bath

Heat the cream and coconut milk for 1 ½ minutes in the microwave or boil on a stove over medium heat

Pour the boiled cream over the chocolate and gently whisk till homogenous

Add half the desiccated coconut and mix well

Refrigerate the mixture for at least 2 hours (up to overnight)

Make balls of equal size and roll them in the remaining desiccated coconut and leave in the fridge to harden

DESSERTS

The recipes in this section are more sophisticated and can be made for parties, on special occasions, or for when you want to give your family a treat. If you are new to baking, I recommend you try these once you have mastered the basic techniques of mixing, whipping and folding, by baking brownies or simple cakes.

EGGLESS CHOCOLATE MOUSSE
Serves 2

A no-brainer crowd pleaser. The fact that it is eggless makes it perfect for large dinners, when guests might have dietary preferences.

200g dark chocolate
75g Amul cream
100g whipping cream

Melt the dark chocolate and Amul cream together in a microwave and keep aside

Whip the cream until firm peaks form

Fold in the whipped cream into the chocolate mixture with a spatula

Set in shot glasses or dessert bowls

Refrigerate for a minimum of 2 hours before serving

CLASSIC CHOCOLATE MOUSSE

Serves 4

This recipe is dedicated to my mother, who taught me how to make it. My brother and I fell in love with chocolate mousse early on, and she would whip it up for us on popular demand.

140g dark chocolate
55g butter
2 eggs, separated
25g castor sugar
1tsp vanilla extract
100g cream, whipped

Melt the dark chocolate and butter together in a microwave and set aside to cool

Start whisking the egg whites. Once they begin to froth, add half the sugar slowly and continue to whisk till you get firm peaks

In a separate bowl, whisk together the egg yolks, vanilla extract and the remaining castor sugar till pale and thick

Pour the cooled chocolate and butter into the egg yolks. Ensure that the chocolate is cool, otherwise you could cook the egg yolk and end up with scrambled chocolate eggs!

Lightly fold in with a spatula the egg whites, followed by the whipped cream, until incorporated

Refrigerate for 4 hours before serving

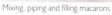

Mixing, piping and filling macarons

Meringues, page 203

PASSION FRUIT WHITE CHOCOLATE MOUSSE

Serves 4

Passion fruit is my absolute favourite fruit. I try and make something with it whenever I can get my hands on some. This white chocolate mousse is very versatile. If you don't find passion fruit you could use fresh strawberries, mangoes, kiwi or even a fruit jam to layer it with. I serve it in a martini glass at home or in small glass jars if I am planning to gift it.

175g white chocolate
2 egg whites
¼tsp lemon juice
225ml whipping cream, whipped
Passion fruit for layering

Melt the white chocolate and milk in a microwave and set aside

Whip the egg whites and lemon juice till stiff, and then fold lightly into the chocolate mixture

Now fold in the whipped cream. Make sure you don't over-mix or you will end up with white chocolate soup

Divide into 4 glasses and layer the mousse with fresh passion fruit (or any fruit of your choice) and chill it for at least 2 hours

STRAWBERRIES AND CREAM
Serves 4

This recipe reminds me of childhood holidays in Mahabaleshwar. The highlight of these holidays was exploring the local market for the nicest strawberry and cream that I could find. And now, at Le15, our jars of strawberry and cream are a big hit.

I use Tropolite whipped cream which is sweetened, so I don't add any sugar. If you are using local fresh cream you could add some sugar while whipping the cream.

150g fresh strawberries
150g cream, whipped

After rinsing the strawberries, cut off the tops and then cut each strawberry in half

Layer a few strawberries in the bottom of a bowl or a jar and then spread some whipped cream on top

Repeat till all the strawberries and whipped cream are used up

Let it set in the fridge for 2 hours and then serve

PASSION FRUIT PAVLOVA

Serves 4

I have already shared my special passion for passion fruit with you, so it must come as no surprise that I am using it again. But you can replace it with any fresh berries or even kiwis. Some things to remember while making pavlova:

Make sure there are no traces of egg yolk when you separate the eggs

While making the meringue, ensure that the bowl is clean and has no grease

Egg whites are delicate and need to be handled with care

Bake at a lower temperature for a longer time to get a nice crust outside and a soft marshmallow-y inside

---

120g castor sugar
1 tbsp cornstarch
3 egg whites
1 tsp vanilla essence
1 tbsp white wine vinegar

Preheat oven. Mix the cornstarch with the castor sugar

In a medium-sized bowl, start whisking the egg whites

Once they start to froth, slowly add the sugar and keep whisking till you get soft peaks

Add the vinegar and vanilla at the end and whisk till the meringue is glossy

Spoon the meringue on to a lined baking tray. Use the back of the spoon to make a dent in the middle of the meringue. This is where you will pour the cream and fruit once the pavlova is baked

Bake at 135C for 45 minutes. Once out of the oven and cool, top with whipped cream and your choice of fresh fruit

CHOCOLATE CHIP PAVLOVA

Serves 4

1 tbsp cornstarch
120g castor sugar
3 egg whites
1 tsp vanilla essence
1 tbsp white wine vinegar
20g cocoa powder
150g chocolate chips

Preheat the oven to 135C

Mix the cornstarch with the castor sugar

In a medium-sized bowl, start whisking the egg whites

Once they start foaming, slowly add the sugar and cornstarch mixture and keep whisking till you get soft peaks

Add the vinegar and vanilla at the end and whisk till the meringue is glossy

Finally add in the cocoa powder and give it a final whisk

Spoon the meringue on to a lined baking tray. Use the back of the spoon to make a dent in the middle of the meringue. This is where you will pour the whipped cream

Bake at 135C for 45 minutes

Once out of the oven and cool, top with whipped cream and chocolate chips

MERINGUES

Makes 40 medium-sized meringues

Meringues are light, airy and perfect for that mid-afternoon sugar rush. They are baked at a lower temperature for a longer time so you get a crusty shell and soft gooey inside. Once you make the meringues you can sandwich them with jam or whipped cream. Plain meringues will last about a week to ten days in an airtight container or 3 weeks if frozen.

120g egg whites
160g castor sugar
A pinch of salt

Preheat the oven to 130C

In a clean bowl, start whisking the egg whites

Once they start to froth, gradually add the castor sugar and salt

Keep whisking till stiff peaks form

Use a piping bag with a star nozzle size 6 or 8 and pipe the meringues on to a lined baking tray

Bake at 135C for 45–50 minutes and once out of the oven, leave it on the tray to cool

MACARONS

I remember the day I ate my first macaron with as much clarity and nostalgia as my graduation day. I stood in line outside a famous Paris pâtisserie for what seemed like an eternity. As I reached the counter I was amazed by the display of colours. I walked out of the store with my very expensive purchase and studied it for a minute. With its glossy surface and skirt it almost looked like a mini burger. I took a bite and felt a rush of flavours playing around in my mouth. The cool tartness of the passion fruit sandwiched within the crisp sweetness of the biscuit—the most beautiful combination I had ever tried!

I was hooked. I moved back to India intent on perfecting the recipe in my kitchen. More than 60 failed recipes and 4 months later I FINALLY found something that worked in my home kitchen.

Macarons are definitely not the easiest of treats to bake and require time and effort. It is a process. You first have to make the filling and then bake the shells. Once the macaron is ready it is essential to leave it in the fridge for a few hours or overnight. Have patience and don't give up.

THE BASIC TRICKS AND TIPS TO REMEMBER WHILE MAKING MACARONS

Use egg whites that are a day old (separate your egg whites and keep them in the fridge overnight)

Use very fine almond powder—resembling fine bread crumbs. You can make your own by blanching almonds, i.e. putting them in boiling water for 5 minutes and then removing the skin, roasting them in the oven at 165C for a brief 5 minutes and then grinding them in a mixer

Make sure to use only castor sugar in your meringue

Depending on the humidity, macarons take time to dry. I recommend piping them on a baking sheet and then allowing them to dry in a warm and dry place in your home

Once you have piped the filling in the shells, sandwich the macarons and store them in the fridge overnight before eating them. The flavour drastically improves with time

BASIC MACARON SHELLS

Makes 20 macarons

Macaron shells do not have any flavour. The entire flavour is in the filling. You can use this basic recipe to make shells of any colour and then choose your filling accordingly. I prefer using liquid colours to gel colours. Gel colours make the shells grainy and patchy. Any liquid food colour that's easily available should work.

(The truffle section will give you lots of filling ideas.) I've included one filling here.

MACARON BATTER
100g powdered sugar
100g almond powder
70g egg whites
65g castor sugar
1 tsp liquid food colouring

Whisk the powdered sugar and almond powder so that there are no lumps

Beat the egg whites and, once they start to froth, add in the castor sugar until you get firm peaks

Mix the stiff egg white meringue and food colouring with the powdered sugar and almond powder. Use a spatula to mix till the batter flows freely

Pipe this batter on to a baking tray lined with parchment paper, in circles around 1-inch wide, evenly spaced 1-inch apart. Set the tray aside for 30 minutes

Bake for 10–12 minutes at 165C

Cool completely before removing from the baking sheet

CHOCOLATE GANACHE FILLING
150g dark chocolate, chopped
90g cream
15g butter

Place the chopped dark chocolate in a stainless steel bowl

Heat the cream in a saucepan over medium heat and bring to a boil

Immediately pour the boiling cream over the chocolate and allow it to stand for 5 minutes

Stir with a whisk till smooth and add in the butter. Let it cool

ASSEMBLY

Pair similar-sized macaron shells together

Pipe the ganache onto one shell from each pair. Do not over-fill or else it will ooze out once sandwiched

Gently press the shells together. Store in an airtight container